LATIN
INSCRIPTIONS
IN OXFORD

LATIN
INSCRIPTIONS
IN OXFORD

✦

INSCRIPTIONES
ALIQUOT
OXONIENSES

COMPILED WITH TRANSLATIONS BY
REGINALD H. ADAMS

Bodleian Library
UNIVERSITY OF OXFORD

This edition first published in 2015 by
the Bodleian Library
Broad Street
Oxford OX1 3BG

www.bodleianshop.co.uk

ISBN 978 1 85124 430 0

First published in 1994 by the Perpetua Press, Oxford,
as *Latin in Oxford*, by Reginald H. Adams

Cover design by Dot Little at the Bodleian Library
Text designed and typeset in 10½ on 12 Monotype Bembo Book
by illuminati, Grosmont
Printed and bound by Page Bros Ltd, Norwich,
on 80 gsm Munken Print Cream

British Library Catalogue in Publishing Data
A CIP record of this publication is available from the British Library

CONTENTS

FILIAE NOSTRAE
CARISSIMAE
RUTH MARGARETAE

FOREWORD

IT IS A CLICHÉ among connoisseurs of Latin that the language has a 'lapidary' quality. It is certainly true that Latin goes very well on stone. The language is capable of extraordinary effects of compression: the absence of words for 'a' and 'the'; the fondness for omitting 'and' and 'but'; the ability to achieve unambiguous sense with very little use of prepositions like 'of' and 'to' and 'with'; the variety of possible forms for verbs, nouns, and adjectives, each with its own precise and transparent grammatical function: such things conspire to create in Latin a weighty and pregnant manner, uncluttered with little auxiliary words, and juxtaposing substantial ones with a minimum of connecting mortar between the massy stones.

It is also the case that we have an enormous number of inscriptions in Latin, on stone and bronze, from the days of classical antiquity—the Romans were great believers in immortalising their doings and great users of inscriptions—and also from the practice of Christians, all the way from the Roman Empire, through the Middle Ages, to the Renaissance and after. An Englishman who went to Rome in the seventeenth or eighteenth century, having spent most of his time at his public school on Latin, found a city dominated by enormous inscriptions set up by the Popes, in Latin as classical as they could make it, recording papal activity and generosity in building and repairing churches, bridges, aqueducts, fountains, and every other feature of the Eternal City.

But it was not only Papists who relished inscriptions in the learned language. So sturdy an Anglican as Samuel Johnson declared that nothing would induce him to dishonour the walls of Westminster Abbey with an epitaph in English. The timeless vehicle of Latin gave dignity and form to fleeting emotions, whether of pride in achievement or grief for the dead. It attached the present moment to the endless pageant of the past, and it avoided the transient, the temporary and the trivial, by borrowing some of the gravity and exploiting the marmoreal restraint of classical writing. Understatement, in the Roman way, is thus part of the armoury of the Latin epitaph writer.

The compiler of this book has done something which many of us have vaguely thought of doing and lazily failed to do. He has assembled with energy and translated and explained with love a choice selection of the Latin inscriptions of Oxford. He has thrown in a few Greek ones, for good measure. May it be said of him, as ancient Romans said of the antiquarian Marcus Varro, that he has for the first time made us feel at home in our own city.

Jasper Griffin, former Public Orator, 1994

EXORDIUM

The purpose of this modest anthology of selected inscriptions is twofold. It aims first to provide examples of the epigraphic records available *in situ* to historians, and secondly to offer a source of interest to the observant passer-by who, intrigued by these evocative mementoes of the past, might attempt to read them if their subject matter were not too highly specialised and some of the problems eased for him or her. To that end fairly literal translations have been provided which will, for example, demonstrate the striking difference in word order between the two languages. In a few cases the composer of modern memorials has kindly offered the English version.

Some difficulty may be encountered from the various abbreviations in use, but this should not be a surprise to a generation which is familiar with acronyms. A list of those commonly found on epitaphs is provided later. The shortening of a word is usually indicated by a full stop, this being sometimes the only form of punctuation to be found on an inscription. For the sake of comprehension I have in most cases restored abbreviated Latin words to their full length. Sadly, the individual design of the inscriptions selected and the work of the *lapicida* (stonecutter) which would best have been conveyed by photography, cannot be captured in type, though it is hoped that the printed form will make them easier to decipher and comprehend. What also is not shown in these examples is the decorative effect of variation in size of lettering, accents for stress and for length of vowels, the diphthongs and ligatures, the apostrophe marks to indicate omission and the horizontal lines above contracted words. Nor has the breaking up of words between lines to make the best use of space available been noted, although some of the texts have been reproduced in the alignment of their originals.*

A few examples in Greek have been included in this selection, which would be the poorer without them. Some inscriptions are in capital letters and some in the more familiar minuscule. Greek verses are occasionally found below a Latin epitaph in a college chapel.

---

* A good general background to the problems of designer and craftsman will be found in G. Susini, The *Roman Stonecutter*, 1973.

These transcriptions and notes owe much to the help of many friends. It would be difficult to list all of them and the compiler hopes it will be understood if he first refers to members of St John Baptist College, to which his personal debt has steadily increased since undergraduate days. His contemporary James Eggleshaw has given generous assistance with inscriptions. Several members of the Fellowship have shown the most encouraging and kindly interest, among them Nicholas Purcell and Donald Russell, Emeritus Professor of Classical Literature, all of whose scholarly guidance has been greatly appreciated.

I am much indebted to Jasper Griffin, the former Public Orator, for his arresting foreword, which will give immense encouragement to teachers of Latin and support its retention in the curriculum. Production has been made the easier by the patient typing of the manuscript by Ruth Forster.

R.H.A., 1994

PRAEFATIO

T HE STATUTES composed by the Scottish princess Dervorguilla in 1282 for the foundation of Balliol College included the requirement that 'our scholars shall commonly speak Latin'. In theory this has remained the official language of the University as codified in the Laudian Statutes. The Chancellor opens Convocation with a preliminary: *'Causa hujus Convocationis est...'* At the beginning of a meeting of Congregation the Senior Proctor seeks permission for the proceedings to continue in English. *'Insignissime Domine Vice-Cancellarie, licetne Anglice loqui?'*

Such concessions to modern procedure have long been desirable, but there has since the twentieth century been a steady decline in the number of those with a background knowledge of the classics. Compulsory Greek was abandoned in 1920, but Latin remained a requirement for matriculation until the abolition in 1960 of Responsions, the name of the old scholastic exercise once commonly known as 'Smalls'. Both tongues remain essential for those reading 'Greats' in the faculty of *Literae Humaniores*. It is still desirable in the faculties of Modern History, of Medieval and Modern Languages and of English to have a background knowledge of Latin, but the proportion of others who have even a limited acquaintance with that language has now been reduced to a small minority. If Oxford is to remain a commonwealth of the *literati*, as the tablet in the Schools Quadrangle records, some appreciation of the legacy of Rome to the life of the university ought to be conveyed to those who study here.

VIVA VOCE

The *Viva* (spoken word) is the colloquial name for an oral examination in the university, and *Lingua Latina* is happily still to be heard in Oxford.

Survivals from the literary past remain in use at matriculation and degree ceremonies—*in matricula* (the register) or *ad gradum* (the degree)—which are compulsory for every would-be graduate. The annual admission of Proctors in the House of Convocation is also conducted wholly in Latin. The skill of the Public Orator in presenting honorands for their degrees at *Encaenia* creates the most interesting event in the university year, and his text with a translation on the facing page of the programme can be followed without difficulty. Latinised equivalents have to be invented to match technical terms or modern experiences and the ancient tongue thereby remains a living language.

The mass is sung in Latin by the congregation on Sundays at the Oxford Oratory (the church of St Aloysius). The *Gloria, Sanctus* and *Benedictus* are likewise sung by the choir during the Eucharist at the cathedral on most Sundays during the year. It is also possible to hear the whole liturgy and to recite the words of the General Confession in Latin at a *Cena Domini* (Supper of the Lord or Holy Communion) in the University Church of St Mary the Virgin, and once a year in January the *Litania* is sung and a 'Latin sermon' is preached there.

Grace before dinner is said daily in Latin at most colleges. At Gaudies members may listen to an *oratio* by a scholar about events in the life of the college during the past year. A Latin refrain—*Caput apri defero reddens laudes Domino*—'I bear the Boar's Head giving praises to the Lord'—is sung at Christmas at The Queen's. The *Hymnus Eucharisticus* is the original May morning chant at the top of the tower of Magdalen.

A new reader, on admission to the Bodleian, may choose to make the declaration in Latin and swear not to bring fire into the Library. The full text is provided as a reminder on one side of a canvas bag with an English translation on the other, on sale in its bookshop.

NOMINA

The titles of many offices in the academic world are of Latin origin and the great majority have been included in the *Oxford English Dictionary*. The style of Proctor comes by contraction from *procurator* (overseer). A few others remain in current college use. *Tutor* (guardian) is the official designation of Fellows directly responsible for the intellectual and moral guidance of undergraduates. The tutor in music, organist and choirmaster at Magdalen is known as *informator choristarum*. The two Students of Christ Church who hold responsibility for disciplinary matters are called *censores* and the *censor theologiae* is the senior member of the governing body concerned with the college rather than the cathedral. At University and at The Queen's a Fellow is also styled *praelector*—'one who reads and explains'. In translation this has provided a national grade in higher education of 'senior lecturer'. Professorial status was originally granted only to those who held an endowed or established *cathedra* (chair), but some recent appointments as *professor* or reader in the university on a personal basis for the lifetime of their holders have been made *ad hominem*. The historic duties of a 'Grammar Reader' have been revived in a *grammatikos* who in the capacity of 'Grocyn Lecturer' teaches Greek to beginners. Undergraduates and nowadays graduates receiving tuition are *in statu pupillari* (pupillage). When they take university examinations they are required to be *suffusci* and wear 'subfusc' (specified dark clothes).

A college, hall or former priory in Oxford is described as *Domus*, referring not only to its buildings, but to those for whom as teachers in the university it provides their 'house' or home. A Master, Warden, Rector, Provost, President or Principal is entitled the 'Head of House', and *Domus* is not infrequently used in various contexts relating to its life and organisation.

Christ Church enjoys a special title—*Aedes Christi*. This makes possible a play on words, since the dual foundation of cathedral and college is colloquially known as 'The House' (of Christ). This becomes even more clear in the abridgement of its Latin name—COLL. AED. XTI. The abbreviation of those of some other colleges may at first sight be unrecognisable—COLL. OM. AN. (*Omnium Animarum*) for All Souls—COLL. AEN. NAS. (*Aenei Nasi*) eponymously for Brasenose—COLL. DI. JO. BAPT, for St John's—COLL. VIG. (*Vigorniense*) for Worcester.

EPITAPHIA MORTUORUM

In Oxford there are inscriptions to be seen on commemorative and foundation stones and on wall plaques, on plinths below statues and in friezes on high. But by far the largest number are eulogies to the deceased. These are more numerous in buildings of the university, but several churches of the city contain memorials to its more noteworthy citizens. One of these churches has now become a chapel for St Peter's, and others make splendid libraries for Lincoln and St Edmund Hall. The chapels, ante-chapels, cloisters and arcades make an impressive environment and there now seems in some colleges little space remaining on their walls, floors and pavements for more obituary inscriptions. Together they provide much interesting first-hand commentary on the life and times of those whom they commemorate.

William Camden (1551–1629), Fellow of Magdalen and Student of Christ Church, suggested that an epitaph should show 'love to the deceased, memory to posterity and comfort to friends'. This advice has generally been followed. Samuel Johnson (1709–1784), who had strong opinions on this subject, admitted that 'in lapidary inscriptions a man is not upon oath'. There is bound to be suspicion that some epitaphs may have been influenced by individuals before their death. Their length ranges from the severely brief to the verbose or even to a *curriculum vitae* (possibly explainable by reasons of financial gain), and the succinct are often the more effective. The present preference is for brevity and simplicity, and much may be expressed in Latin with more economy than in English. Epitaphs in Latin are still appropriate, and, there being no shortage of Latinists in the university, they are being eruditely and effectively composed.

Memorials to the fallen occupy a prominent position in places of education, and Oxford has its full share with long rolls of honour from two world wars. Several colleges have their preference for commemorating their *alumni* in the ancient tongue, in the tradition of *Dulce et decorum est pro patria mori*—'It is gratifying and becoming to die for one's country' (Horace, *Odes* 2.13). The names of the very many Christ Church men who made the supreme sacrifice are inscribed on both sides of the porch leading into the cathedral from Tom Quad. On the north side outside the west door is a prayer above the lists—*Requiem aeternam dona eis, Domine, et lux perpetua luceat eis*—'O Lord, grant them eternal rest and let light perpetual shine upon them'—the Introit to the *Officium defunctorum* (the mass offered for the dead) in the Roman Breviary. Trinity chose to establish a scholarship fund as its memorial to the fallen in the second world war. To keep to a minimum the size of its visible expression of loss on a tablet (1949) on the gates leading to the garden the governing body reduced a longer text to four poignant words—*Suos Domus luget laudat*—'This house mourns her sons and extols them.' There are also some inscriptions in Greek in the college library in memory of those who died in both world wars.

Latin epitaphs and memorials in Oxford serve to reincarnate scholars and statesmen of the past and for older generations to revive friendships of youth—*incisa notis marmora publicis/ per quae spiritus et vita redit bonis/ post mortem ducibus*—'marble graves inscribed with public records, whereby breath and life return to goodly heroes after death' (Horace, *Odes* 4.8.13–15).

EPIGRAMMATA ALIBI COLLOCATA

One inscription appears more frequently in Oxford than any other— the motto of the university. It is heraldically presented on the facing pages of an open book with the three Latin words so divided as to keep a balance on each side. For this reason *Dominus illuminatio mea* may not be easily recognised as the first words of Psalm 27—'The Lord is my Light.' This is probably the oldest of several mottoes which have appeared on the shield of arms of the university. A corresponding open book in the centre of the shield of the cathedral's arms, which were recognised at a visitation in 1574 of Oxfordshire, contains another motto once used by the university—*Principio erat verbum et verbum erat apud Deum*—the opening words of the Gospel according to St John—'In the beginning was the Word and the Word was with God.'*

It would be surprising if Latin were not clearly visible in the heart of the university and a variety of inscriptions on its central buildings will be recorded later. To these must be added the brief words beneath the statue on the west side of the Clarendon Building about Edward Hyde (1609–1674), the first Earl, whose name has become so clearly associated with Oxford and its university press—*Edwardus Comes Clarendon Summus Angliae Summus Academiae*—'Edward Earl of Clarendon, the most exalted of Englishmen, the most respected in the university' (Chancellor from 1660 to 1667). This free rendering

---

* The arms of the cathedral are on display on the left sleeve of the gown of the Dean's verger.

reinforces the point that the Latin language is succinct. Two striking words—*Regnante Carolo*—which are a feature of the hall porch of Oriel with its pierced parapet record the reconstruction of the buildings 'in the reign of King Charles I', which he would have seen when Oxford became the Royalist capital in 1642.

Some of the college buildings of the twentieth century incorporate inscriptions in Latin on foundation stones. The front quadrangle of Hertford has in the cloister of its chapel an account of its dedication by Francis Paget, Bishop of Oxford between 1900 and 1911 *adsistente collegio*, recording the presence of all members of the community in 1907. Bishop Edward Talbot, who when Warden of Keble was chairman of the council which founded Lady Margaret Hall in 1878, laid a commemorative stone on the exterior of the apse of its chapel in 1932, *ad majorem Dei gloriam*—'to the greater glory of God'. A good example of a *lapis angularis* (cornerstone) of 1934 is to be found at the east end of Campion Hall in Brewer Street. A stone had been set in a similar position in 1873 for the *Tabernaculum Dei* (chapel) of St Edward's School.

The chapel is, like hall and library, at the heart of a college. In the front quadrangle of Jesus (1591) the tympanum of the chapel invites those who worship here—*Ascendat Oratio, Descendat Gloria*—'Let prayer go up, let glory come down.' In the latter half of the nineteenth century Latin inscriptions, stimulated by the Oxford Movement, played a major part in the redecoration of the chapels of Pembroke and Worcester, and there was further opportunity for Victorian designers in new city churches and in the chapels at Exeter and Keble. Above a consecration cross (1883) on the exterior of the east end of the chancel of the church of St Margaret is the appropriate wording—*Una pretiosa Margarita*—'One pearl of great price' (Matthew 13.46). Mansfield (1889), the first nonconformist college in Oxford, displays its motto over the main entrance—*Deus locutus est nobis in Filio*—'God has spoken to us in his Son' (Hebrews 1.2). Over the door of the interdenominational chapel of Somerville (1935) is an inscription in Greek capital letters—ΟΙΚΟΣ ΠΡΟΣΕΥΧΗΣ ΠΑΣΙ ΤΟΙΣ ΕΘΝΕΣΙΝ—declaring it to be 'a house of prayer for all peoples' (Isaiah 56.7). The same theme appears over the porch of the chapel at Hertford—*Domus mea, Domus orationis*—'My house shall be a house of prayer' (Luke 19.46). At the west end of the modern church

(1954) in New Marston dedicated to St Michael and All Angels their joyous message can be clearly read—*Gloria in altissimis Deo et in terra pax*—'Glory to God in the highest and peace on earth' (Luke 2.14).

There is a humanist message at the heart of the Science area where bold lettering on the top of the north facade at the rear of the former Dyson Perrins Laboratory (now the Oxford University Centre for the Environment)—*Alchymista spem alit aeternam*—expresses the belief that 'scientific experiment keeps hope alive for ever'. Green Templeton College can now be proud of the display of the Greek names for the winds visible beneath the eight reliefs which adorn the summit of the Radcliffe Observatory (1794), inspired by the Tower of the Winds at Athens.

Another lofty but much abbreviated inscription has been set by Magdalen in the concrete summit of the Waynflete building (1960) facing the college on the other side of the bridge. It can be expanded to read: 'The College of the Blessed Mary Magdalen erected this building through the generosity of its former members in honour of our founder William Waynflete some five hundred years ago.' This was in response to a charitable appeal by the college. One of the city's ancient charities in the original sense of good works and alms-giving still produces support for the parish of St Thomas the Martyr, where it originated. A footnote to a monument to the Kendall family in the church records that as a result of a bequest before the death in 1715 of Anne, a youngest daughter—*beneficientiae et eleemosynarum suavissimum odorem sera usa ad saecula transmisit*—'the milk of human kindness and mercy conveyed the sweetest savour for ever'.

The many fine examples of stained glass in Oxford represent almost every style and period in the painting of glass. They also illustrate the history and teaching of the Church with inscriptions in Latin and quotations from the Bible, and historical figures are identifiable by their names. The fine series of windows by Abram van Linge in the chapel of Lincoln (1630) is accompanied by the relevant verses beneath from the Vulgate. Around the hall of New College there is in a frieze beneath the windows a selection of graces for use at meals in the latter half of the nineteenth century.[*]

---

[*] *Vide* R.H. Adams, *The College Graces of Oxford and Cambridge* (Bodleian, 2013), pp. 20–21.

At the end of the last century too the city's historic motto—*Fortis est veritas*—'Strong is the truth'—was set beneath the clock at Carfax Tower and, following the lead of the university, short epigraphs appeared on Victorian civic buildings. Those who entered the courts by the side entrance of the Town Hall could read words above from Virgil (*Aeneid* 6.620)—*Discite justitiam moniti*—'Be warned and learn justice.' Above the entrance to the Old Fire Station in George Street, and more easily understood, the Oxford Volunteer Fire Brigade was described as *Semper paratus, semper volens*—'always ready, always willing'. Meanwhile the university had inscribed on its splendid new premises in St Giles for the teaching of European languages—*Institutio Tayloriana*, and a long inscription in Sanskrit is still to be seen inside the entrance of the former Indian Institute building on the corner of Broad Street and Holywell Street.

The Ashmolean Museum—*Musaeum Ashmoleanum apud Oxonienses*—provides this university city with excellent opportunities to see examples of inscriptions from the classical world. There is to be found among the Roman antiquities an amusing memorial to a sausage seller, a member of the Jewish community in Rome in the third or fourth century A D, which contains some surprising 'howlers' of which native speakers were capable. The Heberden Coin Room has examples on view from its vast collection of inscribed Greek and Roman money.

Marks & Spencer have preserved an unusual triangular boundary stone—*lapidem sacrum*—'sacred' because it was set up to mark the point where some of the city parishes meet. Its exact original position is marked with a cross on the eastern side of the ground floor of the store in Queen Street, and the stone itself is well displayed in a corner of the wall some ten yards away by the side of the customer lift. Each Ascension Day the store is visited by one of the processions 'beating the bounds'.

Inscriptions in Latin above or beneath some historic portraits provide useful means of identification. In the seventeenth century these were occasionally embellished with verses or a motto to accompany a coat of arms. A tablet attached to the frame of a portrait of Sir Thomas Bodley on view in the Bodleian Library urges the visitor not to depart without gazing upon this 'Maecenas of the Muses'. The portrait of Elias Ashmole in the Ashmolean displays

Praemia honoraria, medals and chains which are displayed on his person.

The series of reproduced maps of the city which began with the illustration of Elizabethan Oxford by Ralph Agas in 1588 contain much descriptive material in Latin about the university and the city. Such texts were further developed in *Oxonia Illustrata* (1675) by David Loggan, a bird's-eye view of each of the colleges and of the university buildings.

Sundials often carry brief messages. Beneath the splendid dial which Sir Christopher Wren designed in 1659 for the exterior of the chapel of All Souls, later transferred to its present setting above a central entrance to the Codrington Library, are the words—*pereunt et imputantur*—'Our days pass away and are scored to our account' (Martial, *Epigrammata* 5.20.13). On the upper floor of the Old Ashmolean, which has a particularly fine collection of heraldic glass with Latin inscriptions, is a window dial proclaiming—*Vesper in ambiguo est*—'The evening is at twilight'—and urging—*Age dum, mora noxia, cras nil*—'Do it now. Delay is dangerous, tomorrow does not exist.'

Latin is not normally found in English novels, but the concluding words of *Gaudy Night* by Dorothy L. Sayers (1935), which was then described as 'the best picture of contemporary Oxford life', brings to mind for many the magic of a summer evening. *Placetne, Magistra?*— was a proposal of marriage by Lord Peter Wimsey in New College Lane. The reply was—*Placet*, the word used for agreement in voting in Congregation today. Lord Peter and his fiancée would, as detectives, have enjoyed an inscription on the front of a bench set on a footpath in Merton land near 'Mesopotamia'—*Ore stabit fortis arare placet ore stat*. The meaning is baffling until rearrangement of the gaps between the letters reveals that these can be English words as well as Latin. Not only is it a puzzle to read; it is a puzzle to find.*

---

* The trail begins at Linacre in South Parks Road. In about 300 yards the cycle path to Marston crosses Holywell Mill Stream. After a few paces turn right through an iron gate and without crossing the next bridge follow closely the west bank of the River Cherwell for about half a mile. A solid (third) wooden bench on the way offers on its rim the promised rest.

INSCRIPTIONUM SYLLOGAE
ANTEHAC CONFECTAE

The collecting of inscriptions both in the city and the university, which was begun by Anthony Wood (1632–1695) and brought up to date by the Revd John Gutch (1746–1831), the Registrar of the university (1797–1824), provides impressive examples of accurate recording under difficult conditions. In this century complete catalogues have been made for the brass and lapidary inscriptions in four college chapels and for some fifty brasses in the cathedral, but translations have not previously been included.*

It would be an exercise expensive in effort and cost to continue the work of transcription of so many more in all colleges and in churches, of which the number steadily grows, but the task so well begun might happily then end with a complete Oxonian record.

EXEMPLARUM COLLECTIO

Oxford as the seat of one of the two ancient universities can claim to be the English city in which inscriptions in Latin are the most numerous and probably the most interesting. Despite the inevitable loss of some as the result of much rebuilding before their historical importance was appreciated it is hardly possible to walk in the historic centre today without seeing some Latin. The general standard of preservation of the remaining memorials in Oxford is praiseworthy, and it is only on gravestones or paving that there is risk of erasure from the tramp of feet.

It has not been easy to make a selection, but the touchstone of visibility has limited this small collection to inscriptions in public places. The combined search for brevity and simplicity has also

---

* A. Wood, *Historiae et Antiquitates Universitatis Oxoniensis*, 1688; J. Gutch, *The History and Antiquities of the Colleges and Halls in the University of Oxford*, 1786; A. Clark (ed.), *Survey of the Antiquities of Oxford, compiled in 1661–6 by A. Wood*, Oxford Historical Series Vols I & III, 1899–1909; C.B. Heberden, *Inscriptions on College Monuments in the Brasenose Register*, Vol. II, pp. 169–89, 1909; R.T. Gunther, *A Description of Brasses and Other Funeral Monuments in the Chapel of Magdalen College, Oxford*, 1914; F.E. Hutchinson and Sir Edmund Craster, *Monumental Inscriptions in the Chapel of All Souls College, Oxford*, 1949; A. Bolt, *The Monuments in Merton College Chapel*, 1962; J. Arthur, *A Guide to the Memorial Brasses in Christ Church, Oxford*, 1990.

resulted in the exclusion of many interesting inscriptions, which will disappoint those whose favourites have been omitted. Perhaps the eye seeking one text may light on others in the vicinity. It is hoped that the result is a representative collection with a balance between academic and civic, epitaphic and historical, and past and present. The cathedral is unusually rich in epitaphs to famous men, and Christ Church is strongly represented by its own. The series of memorials engraved on brass, of which there are a few examples in the selection, and some outstanding monuments relating to English history and literature make this college a particularly rewarding place for exploration. The search elsewhere in Oxford for contemporary Latinity to commemorate occasions worthy of note can prove equally satisfying.

The buildings of the university come first in the order of selection, with the colleges in alphabetical order. These are followed by a civic section, which includes the ancient churches of the city.

PERLUSTRATE SION ET CIRCUITE EAM,
NUMERATE TURRES EIUS.
CONSIDERATE PROPUGNACULA EIUS,
PERCURRITE ARCES EIUS
UT ENARRETIS GENERATIONI FUTURAE.

Walk about Zion and go round about her;
tell the towers hereof.
Mark ye well her bulwarks, scan her peaks
that ye may tell the generation following.

Psalm 48.12–13

EXEMPLA

THE BODLEIAN LIBRARY
THE SCHOOLS QUADRANGLE

The Quadrangle, which was built as an extension of the Bodleian Library between 1612 and 1619, has a display of inscriptions which spell out in detail the curriculum of medieval education in Oxford. Over ten doors which lead into specialist teaching rooms are the Latin titles of separate subjects of study.

There were two preliminary series of lectures—the *trivium* (a liberal three-way course) which consisted of Grammar, Logic and Rhetoric. The *quadrivium* (a mathematical four-way course) included the subjects of Music, Arithmetic, Geometry and Astronomy. Together these courses formed 'seven liberal arts'. To these were added the three philosophies—moral, metaphysical and natural—and two tongues—Greek and Hebrew. All can be clearly identified in the quadrangle.

On the west side of the quadrangle were the schools of the three superior faculties of theology, medicine and law. A central doorway leads through the *Proscholium* (in front of the Schools) to the *Schola theologiae* (Divinity School). On either side are to be seen the former entrances to the *Schola vetus medicinae* (on the left) and the *Schola vetus jurisprudentiae* (on the right).

The other apartments now provide offices for the administration of the library and for meetings of the Curators. Thirty years after their erection they had served the needs of the Royalist army as accommodation for the stores of the quartermaster. In course of time they became inadequate for teaching and examination purposes, and for the latter a replacement building in the High Street was completed in 1882. The new Examination Schools preserved the use of the old name of the quadrangle and provided the title —'Schools', by which examinations in Oxford are known today. The tradition of Latin designations was continued in this building with *Schola magna australis* (south), *Schola magna borealis* (north) and *Schola magna orientalis* (east) for the great 'writing' schools on the first floor.

Above the main entrance to the Library on the west side beneath the Arms of the University and those of Sir Thomas Bodley:

QUOD FELICITER VORTAT
ACADEMICI OXONIENS
BIBLIOTHECAM HANC
VOBIS REIPUBLICAEQUE
LITERATORUM
T.B.P.

May it turn out happily.
Masters of Oxford,
Thomas Bodley placed this library here for you
and for the commonwealth of the educated.

The west range of the quadrangle was completed in 1612 by an extension to Duke Humfrey's Library of its Arts End, with the *Proscholium* beneath.

This dedicatory inscription was no doubt composed by Sir Thomas Bodley to emphasise that this was from the first intended as a public library. His initials followed by P (*posuit*) confirm this.

The *Oxford English Dictionary* defines a Republic of Letters (cf. *La république des lettres*) as the collective body of those engaged in literary pursuits. *Literatus* was used classically to describe someone learned or liberally educated.

The text of the inscription is interesting in other respects. Its first line is a conventional expression of good wishes, which will be found elsewhere in this collection. Although there is no stop to indicate this, the last word of the second line has been abbreviated from *Oxonienses*, which would have been appropriate in its vocative plural form. This lends shape to the inscription. The letters of the middle line have been enlarged and *Bibliothecam* given prominence. The two words *res* (the state) and *publica* are used in combination and declined as one word in the dative case.

3

On a panel below the figure of King James I
on the fourth storey of the tower on the east side:

REGNANTE D. JACOBO REGUM DOCTISSIMO
MUNIFICENTISSIMO OPTIMO HAE MUSIS
EXTRUCTAE MOLES CONGESTA BIBLIOTHECA
ET QUAECUNQUE ADHUC DEERANT AD SPLENDOREM
ACADEMIAE FELICITER TENTATA
COEPTA ABSOLUTA. SOLI DEO GLORIA

In the reign of the Lord James, of kings the most learned, the most
generous and the best, this massive tower was erected for the Muses,
the library was gathered together and whatsoever was hitherto
lacking for the magnificence of the university was
successfully planned, begun and completed.
To God alone be the glory.

Sir Thomas Bodley had suggested the rebuilding of the old Schools in
a new quadrangle with a gallery above and he left money in his will
for this purpose. It was designed to include on the east side a large
gatehouse—probably through the influence of his friend, Sir Henry
Savile, the Warden of Merton, where such an addition had quite
recently been made. This monument came to be known as the Tower
of the Five Orders of Architecture, (Doric, Tuscan, Ionic, Corinthian
and Composite). Before its completion in 1619 an inscription was set
beneath an effigy of an enthroned King James I presenting copies
of his published works to female figures representing Fame and the
university. These may have included the Authorised Version of the
Bible, which was published in 1611 and which is sometimes known as
the 'King James' version. On a canopy above the effigy are the words
from the Beatitudes—*Beati pacifici* —'Blessed are the peacemakers'
(Matthew 5.9).

The archives of the university together with the records of the
Vice-Chancellor's Court were transferred to the highest room of the
tower in the middle of the nineteenth century.

On two sides of the plinth below the life-sized bronze
statue by Hubert Le Sueur of William Herbert:

GULIELMUS PEMBROCHIAE COMES
REGNANTIBUS JACOBO ET CAROLO PRIMIS
HOSPITII REGII CAMERARIUS
ET SENESCAILUS ACADEMIAE OXONIENSIS
CANCELLARIUS MUNIFICENTISSIMUS

HANC
PATRUI SUI MAGNI EFFIGIEM
AD FORMAM QUAM PINXIT PETRUS PAULUS RUBENS
AERE FUSO EXPRESSAM
ACADEMIAE OXONIENSI D.D.
THOMAS PEMBROCHIAE ET MONTGOM. COMES
HONORUM ET VIRTUTUM HAERES
A.D. MDCCXXIII

*William, Earl of Pembroke, Chamberlain and Steward of the
Royal Household in the reign of James I and Charles I, and most
munificent Chancellor of the University of Oxford.*

*Thomas, Earl of Pembroke and Montgomery, inheritor of his titles
and qualities, presented as a gift to Oxford University this statue of
his great uncle in the form which Peter Paul Rubens had depicted,
which was then cast in bronze. A.D. 1723.*

This inscription was placed upon the plinth when the statue was
transferred from the family home at Wilton. The text as reproduced
above begins on the reverse side of the plinth.

William, the 3rd Earl, after whom the college of Pembroke was
named, was Chancellor of the University from 1616 until his death in
1630. A painted inscription had been placed in his honour above the
entrance to the passage on the south side of the quadrangle at the time
of its completion in 1624. Below is the Pembroke coat of arms and the
Herbert motto in Old French —*Ung je serveray*—'One I will serve.'

THE BODLEIAN LIBRARY
STAIRCASE

At the top of the staircase leading to the entrance to Arts End:

THE BENEFACTORS' TABLET

beneath the Arms of Sir Thomas Bodley:

NE TANTORUM BENEFICIORUM MEMORIA OBSOLESCAT
HIC GRATO ANIMO INSCRIBIT ACADEMIA NOMINA
EORUM QUI MUNERIBUS SUIS
HANC BIBLIOTHECAM MAGNIFICE AUXERUNT

Lest the memory of such great benefactions should fade away
the university gratefully inscribes here the names of those who
with their gifts have made splendid additions to this library.

and below the names of benefactors beginning with *Humphredus Dux*
Gloucestriae:

PLURIMI PERTRANSIBUNT ET MULTIPLEX
ERIT SCIENTIA

Many shall run to and fro, and knowledge shall be increased.
(Daniel 12.4, translation from the Authorised Version of 1611)

This tablet was unveiled by the Vice-Chancellor on 23 January 1923
as a visible counterpart to the 'Register Booke' of benefactors, which
Thomas Bodley began in June 1600, before the library was formally
opened to readers. A second tablet has now been added.

Much running 'to and fro' is inevitable in a large library, but it
is possible that this is a metaphorical reference to the study of the
scriptures. There can be no such doubt about the prophecy concerning
the many aspects of learning.

The names of benefactors appear in their Latinised form as far as
possible. Two are shown as having held the office of *Protobibliothecarius*
(Bodley's Librarian).

THE BODLEIAN LIBRARY
DUKE HUMFREY'S LIBRARY

On the left of the entrance from Arts End
beneath the portrait bust:

THOMAS SACKVILLUS DORSET. COMES
SUMMUS ANGLIAE THESAURAR. ET
HUJUS ACAD. CANCELLAR.
THOMAE BODLEIO EQUITI AURATO
QUI BIBLIOTHECAM HANC INSTITUIT
HONORIS CAUSA P.P.

*Thomas Sackville Earl of Dorset, Lord High Treasurer of England
and Chancellor of this university placed this bust in honour of
Sir Thomas Bodley, who founded this library.*

Thomas Sackville (1536–1608) was Chancellor of the university from
1591 until his death. This wall monument, said to be an excellent
likeness, was set in position in 1605, the year after Sir Thomas Bodley
received the honour of Knighthood. He had the experience of looking
at his own memorial during the eight remaining years of his life.

Arts End was added to Duke Humfrey's Library during the
lifetime of the founder. It was so named because it housed books,
as it still does, in subjects of study other than those in the main
disciplines, which remained in 'Duke Humfrey', Hence 'Arts' became
their comprehensive title and provided the names for the main degrees
of the university.

For reasons of security, inspection of the above inscription and that
on the previous page is possible only for readers with a pass to the
Library and for those on the special Bodleian guided tours.

THE BODLEIAN LIBRARY
DIVINITY SCHOOL

THE DRAKE CHAIR

SELLA EX RELIQUIIS TABULATORUM NAVIS DRACANAE
FABRICATA ET A JOHANNE DAVISIO DEPTFORDIENSI
ARM. NAVALIUM ARMAMENTORUM CUSTODE REGIO
BIBLIOTHECAE OXONIENSI DEDICATA 1662

This chair, made from the timbers of Sir Francis Drake's ship,
when it was broken up, was given to the Bodleian Library at
Oxford in 1662 by John Davies, Gentleman, of Deptford,
Warden of the Royal Dockyards.

Abraham Cowley (1618–1667) was a Scholar and Fellow of Trinity
College Cambridge until he was ejected in 1644 and came to study
at St John's College Oxford, which he left before the surrender of
the Royalist capital to accompany the Queen to Paris. On a second
visit to Oxford he received the degree of Doctor of Medicine on 2
December 1657.

He composed in 1662 commemorative verses in both languages
for the occasion of the gift of the Drake Chair. These are attached
to the back in a suspended tablet, Latin on one side and English on
the other. The concluding four lines are as follows:

NON POTERAT MERITIS TRIBUI NAVIQUE DRACIQUE
NOBILIUS PRETIUM, NOBILIORVE LOCUS.
NAM SEDET AETERNA COMPOSTUS UTERQUE QUIETE,
ET DRACUS IN CAELO NAVIS ET OXONII

Drake and his Ship, could not have wished from Fate
A more blest Station, or more blest Estate.
For Lo, a Seate of endless Rest is given
To her in Oxford, and to him in Heaven.

At least three other similar chairs are known to exist.

Exterior, the ceiling of the canopy over the
doorway opposite the Sheldonian Theatre:

An open book bears on two facing pages a quotation from the Greek
New Testament (Luke 2.46).

εὗρον αὐτὸν καθεζόμνον ἐν μέσῳ τῶν διδασκάλων

They found him sitting in the midst of the Doctors.

In 1669 Sir Christopher Wren designed this additional entrance
doorway into the fifteenth-century building to allow processions
to robe and be formed up in the Divinity School, thence to pass
into the theatre opposite, of which he had become architect in 1663,
when Savilian Professor of Astronomy. His monogram CWA (for
Christopher Wren architect) on the canopy is repeated in the interior
of the building.

THE SHELDONIAN THEATRE

On its north semi-circular facade:

ACADEMIAE OXONIENSI BONISQUE LITERIS S. GILBERTUS
SHELDON ARCHIEP. CANTUARIENSIS CANCELLAR.
UNIVERS. FECIT A.D. CIƆIƆCLXVIII*

*Dedicated to the University of Oxford and to good learning
Gilbert Sheldon, Archbishop of Canterbury, Chancellor
of the University, built this in 1668.*

Gilbert Sheldon (1598–1677) was Archbishop from 1663 until his death
and Chancellor 1667–1669. He met the entire cost and gave his name
to the building. The theatre is the scene of an annual commemoration
known as *Encaenia*, a Greek word ἐγκαίνια (rededication).

---

* For an explanation of this unusual form of dating see p. 75.

9

THE BODLEIAN LIBRARY
THE WESTON LIBRARY

On the curved wall facing Broad Street:

AEDIFICII NOVI BODLEIANI
HUNC PRIMUM LAPIDEM
POSUIT MARIA REGINA
REGIS GEORGII VI MATER
DIE XXV MENS. JUN. A.D. MCMXXXVII

On 25 June 1937 Queen Mary, the mother of King George VI,
laid this first stone of the New Bodleian.

On the readers' entrance from Blackwell Hall:

SI BONUS ES INTRES: SI NEQUAM NE QUAQUAM

If you are good, enter: if wicked, by no means.

In the vestibule within the entrance in Parks Road:

CUSTODIBUS PECUNIAE EX MANDATO JOHANNIS
DAVIDSON ROCKEFELLER COMMUNI HOMINUM BONO
DEDICATAE SIMUL ET CETERIS QUORUM MUNIFICENTIA
HOC AEDIFICIUM FELICITER EXSTRUCTUM EST GRATA
MEMORIA BIBLIOTHECAE BODLEIANAE CURATORES
A.S. MCMXL

The curators of the Bodleian Library [have placed this]
in grateful acknowledgement to the trustees of the money dedicated
to the common good of mankind in accordance with the will of
John Davidson Rockefeller, and also to the others by whose
munificence this building has successfully been completed.

Fundatio Rockefellerana was also included in the Benefactors' Tablet as
the first of the great charitable trusts to support the Bodleian Library.
    The New Bodleian was formally opened by King George VI and
Queen Elizabeth on 24 October 1946. It reopened to readers in 2014
as the Weston Library.

MUSEUM OF THE
HISTORY OF SCIENCE

WITHOUT

At the foot of the external staircase, visible through gates when closed:

SCALAS LAPIDEAS
ANTE ANNIS PAULO MINUS C. DIRUTAS
SUO SUMPTU RESTITUENDAS CURAVIT
A.S. MCMLVII
JACOBUS ALBERTUS BILLMEIER
NAVICULARIUS
EXCELLMI. ORD. IMP. BRITANNICI
COMMENDATOR
QUOD BENE VERTAT
SCIENTIARUM HISTORIAM ADEUNTIBUS

James Albert Billmeier, Commander of the Most Excellent Order of the British Empire, Shipowner, restored in 1957 at his own expense the stone flight of stairs, which had been in disrepair for nearly a century for the convenience of those approaching the History of Science.

WITHIN

On the main staircase are three notices indicating the original plans for the use of the building in 1683:

on the entry floor   SCHOLA NATURALIS HISTORIAE
the contents of which were transferred to the University Museum in 1860

on the upper floor   MUSEUM ASHMOLEANUM
the contents of which were transferred in 1845 to the new University Galleries

in the basement   OFFICINA CHIMICA
the first university laboratory which was replaced by the 'Glastonbury Kitchen' near the University Museum in 1860 as the beginning of a new science area.

In a west window on the upper half landing of the staircase, four famous seventeenth-century names connected with the building:

UPPER LEFT

JOHANNES TRADESCANT
QUOS ARBUSTA JUVANT CELEBRANT HUNC VIRGINIENSES.
AUSPICE QUO NOSTRIS SUA FRONS INNASCITUR HORTIS

*The people of Virginia, whose delight is in trees, celebrate
John Tradescant, under whose inspiration the foliage that was his
springs up in our gardens.* [1926]

John Tradescant the elder (1570–1638), was in 1637 appointed Keeper of the Physic Garden in Oxford, but he died in the following year. He was a friend of John Smith, the first Governor of Virginia, and his son John Tradescant the younger (1608–1662), to whom this inscription refers, visited the colony to collect plants and shells, which were added to the Tradescant 'Closet of Rareties', also known as 'The Ark'.

UPPER RIGHT

ROBERTUS PLOT R.S.S.
HUIC CELEBRANT CUJUS COLLEGIA NOMEN ET ARTEM
TRADITA MUSAEI EST PRIMO CUSTODIA PRIMI

*Robert Plot, Fellow of the Royal Society.
His colleges celebrate his name and skill.
He was the first Keeper of the first museum.* [1927]

Robert Plot (1640–1696) served as the first Keeper of the first public museum in England until he left Oxford in 1690. He held the appointment of Professor of Chemistry in the university at the same time and established the laboratory in the basement of the building. His colleges were Magdalen Hall and University College, whose shields feature in the window.

ELIAE ASHMOLE
HUJUS MUSEI FUNDATORI
COLL: AEN: NAS: PRINCIPALIS
ET SOCII ALUMNO SUO
HANC FENESTRAM DEDICAVERUNT
MCMXXV

*In 1925 the Principal and Fellows of Brasenose College
dedicated this window to Elias Ashmole, founder of this museum
and a member of their society.*

Elias Ashmole (1617–1692) an attorney with strong interests in herald-
ry and antiquarianism, gave great encouragement to the foundation
of the museum, the contents of which moved to the new Ashmolean
Museum on Beaumont Street in 1908. A cartouche of his arms is also
to be found within the pediment of the main door, and his heraldic
interests are reflected in the display in the windows.

ARCHITECTORUM BRITANNICORUM
CHRISTOPHERUM WREN
ASTRONOMIAE PROFESSOREM
SAVILIANUM CAELESTIBUS EXSTRUCTIONIBUS
NOBILEM COMMEMORANT REGALIS SOCIETAS
MCMXXVII

*In 1927 the Royal Society of British Architects
remember Christopher Wren, Savilian Professor of Astronomy,
renowned for his heavenly constructions.*

Sir Christopher Wren (1632–1723), who entered Wadham College as a
fellow commoner in 1640, was elected to a probationary fellowship at
All Souls in 1653 and was the Savilian Professor of Astronomy when
he embarked on another career with the design of the Sheldonian
Theatre (1669).

In the south window on the lower half landing on the staircase:

LUDOVICUS EVANS D.SC.
QUI MUSEUM ASHMOLEANUM DENUO
LOCUPLETAVIT INSTRUMENTIS NATURALIS
SCIENTIAE COLLATIS HIC COMMEMORATUR

Lewis Evans, Doctor of Science,
who enriched the Ashmolean Museum anew
with his collection of scientific instruments,
is remembered here. [1925]

Lewis Evans (1853–1930) was the founding benefactor of the Museum of the History of Science. For a time his exhibits were known as the 'Lewis Evans Collection'.

INSTAURATIS SCIENTIARUM HISTORIAE STUDIIS
ET ROBERTO GUNTHER LECTORI PRIMO
FENESTRAM DEDICAVERUNT MUSEI VETERIS AMICI

The friends of the 'Old Museum' dedicated this window to
the revived studies of the history of Science and its first Reader,
Robert Gunther.

Robert Gunther (1869–1940), who was also Curator from 1924 to 1940, formed an association of Friends of the Old Museum in 1928.

MUSEI ARMARIA INSTRUXIT ET ARCAM DITAVIT
GILDARUM LONDINIENSIUM LIBERALITAS
QUARUM INSIGNIA DEPINGENDA CURAVIT
MCMXXIX

*The liberality of the London Guilds, whose arms it has enabled
to be displayed, has refurbished the Closets and enriched the Ark.
1929.*

ASPICE IN HAC FENESTRA DEPICTA
CETERARUM SOCIETATUM INSIGNIA
QUAE MUSEUM ANTIQUUM MUNIFICENTIA
RENOVANDUM CURAVERUNT

*See in this window the arms of the other City Companies
which have contributed generously to the restoration
of this ancient museum.*

The City Companies represented in the left-hand window are the *Aurifabri* (Goldsmiths), the *Piscinarii* (Fishmongers), the *Ferrones* (Ironmongers), and the *Tellarii* (Clothworkers). The right-hand window displays the coats of arms of three other companies—the *Merceri* (Mercers), the *Grossarii* (Grocers) and the *Mercatores Scissores* (Merchant Taylors). Below these are the arms of *Coll. Reg. Med.* (The Royal Society of Medicine).

THE ASHMOLEAN MUSEUM
OF ART AND ARCHAEOLOGY

On the great staircase:

HAS AEDES
MILLE STERLINGORUM LIBRIS TESTAMENTO RELICTIS
AUSPICATUS EST
VIR REVERENDUS FRANCIS RANDOLPH S.T.P.
AULAE SANCTI ALBANI PRINCIPALIS
SUIS DEINDE SUMPTIBUS ABSOLVIT
ACADEMIA OXONIENSIS
ANNO SACRO
CIƆ IƆ CCC XLV*

*The Revd Francis Randolph, Doctor of Divinity,
Principal of St Alban's Hall, inaugurated these galleries with the sum left
in his will of a thousand pounds, and the University of Oxford later
completed it at its own expense. 1845.*

On two marble candelabra at the end of the Randolph Gallery:

ACADEMIAE OXONIENSI
HOC ROMANAE ELEGANTIAE EXEMPLAR
EX RUDERIBUS VILLAE
IMPERATORIS HADRIANAE TIBURTINAE
NUPER EFFOSSUM
ROGERUS NEWDIGATE BARONETTUS
GRATO ANIMO D.D.D.
A.D. MDCCLXXVI

*Sir Roger Newdigate, Baronet, gave to the University of Oxford in
gratitude in 1776 this example of Roman elegance recently recovered
from the ruins of the villa of the Emperor Hadrian at Tivoli.*

The two ancient candelabra had been restored in 1769 from Roman
fragments of the second century AD in the workshops of Giambattista
Piranesi (1720–1778).

---

* For an explanation of this unusual form of dating see p. 75.

In the Heberden Coin Room:

This beautiful coin was struck at the Oxford Mint in New Inn Hall by Thomas Rawlins in 1644 during the period when Oxford was the Royalist capital. In the centre of the obverse side the King is mounted on a charger, with a distant view of the City between the legs of the horse. The tower could be that of Magdalen College and one of the spires that of St Mary the Virgin. In the streets are houses of similar shape, and there appear to be walls and defences above marsh land.

Economy of space through abbreviation is well illustrated on coinage. The diameter of the coin is an inch and a half, the size of subsequent commemoration crown pieces.

Obverse, in an outer circle:

CAROLUS D.G. MAG. BRIT. FRAN. ET HIBER. REX
[CAROLUS DEI GRATIA MAGNAE BRITANNIAE
FRANCIAE ET HIBERNIAE REX]

Charles, by the grace of God, King of Great Britain, France and Ireland

Reverse, in an outer circle:

EXURGAT DEUS   DISSIPENTUR INIMICI

Let God arise   Let his enemies be scattered   (Psalm 68.1)

And in the centre:

RELIG · PROT · LEG · ANG · LIBER · PARL · 1644 OXON
[RELIGIO PROTESTANTIUM LEGES ANGLIAE LIBERTAS PARLIAMENTI]

The Religion of Protestants   The Laws of England
The Liberty of Parliament   1644 at Oxford

The King had made a declaration at Oxford in 1642 to support all these. A similar inscription to that on the obverse side appears on the south (semicircular) front of the Sheldonian Theatre with the addition of FID. DEF. (*Fidei Defensor*—Defender of the Faith).

RHODES HOUSE

On the south front along the parapet:

DOMUS HAEC NOMEN ET EXEMPLUM
CECILI JOHAN̄IS RHODES*
OXONIAE QUAM DILEXIT IN PERPETUUM COMMENDAT

This house stands forever as a reminder to the Oxford he loved
of the name and example of Cecil John Rhodes.

On the floor of the lobby of the main entrance:

ΜΗΔΕΙΣ ΚΑΠΝΟΦΟΡΟΣ ΕΙΣΙΤΩ

Let no one who is smoke-bearing enter here.

This is a parody of an inscription supposedly over the door of Plato's
Academy—'Let no one who is not a mathematician enter here.' The
incised words suffer from the inevitable tread of many feet.

On a roundel over the door from the Vestibule to the Rotunda:

NON OMNIS MORIAR

I shall not wholly die. (Horace, *Odes* 3.30)

Around the dome of the Rotunda:

ΤΟ ΑΝΘΡΩΠΙΝΟΝ ΑΓΑΘΟΝ ΨΥΧΗΣ ΕΝΕΡΓΕΙΑ ΓΙΝΕΤΑΙ
ΚΑΤ ΑΡΕΤΗΝ ΕΙ ΔΕ ΠΛΕΙΟΥΣ ΑΙ ΑΡΕΤΑΙ ΚΑΤΑ ΤΗΝ
ΑΡΙΣΤΗΝ ΚΑΙ ΤΕΛΕΙΟΤΑΤΗΝ ΕΤΙ Δ ΕΝ ΒΙΩΙ ΤΕΛΕΙΩΙ

Human good turns out to be an activity of the soul in accordance with
excellence and if there is more than one excellence in accordance with the
best and most complete. But we must add 'in a complete life'.
(Aristotle, *The Nicomachean Ethics* 1.7.15)

Aristotle's definition of happiness is said greatly to have influenced
Rhodes' life and actions. There is another reference to Cecil Rhodes
on page 51. Rhodes House was opened in 1929 as his memorial.

---

* The line above the N indicates contraction from a double N, owing to limited space.

UNIVERSITY MUSEUM
OF NATURAL HISTORY

Immediately on the left of the second entrance door to the museum:

MUSEUM OXONIENSE
NATURALIS SCIENTIAE STUDIO ET DOCTRINAE
CONFIRMANDAE CAUSA CONDITUM
STRUXERUNT
THOMAS DEANE EQUES THOMAS N DEANE
BENJAMIN WOODWARD ARCHITECTI
HUNC PRIMUM OPERIS POSTERIS PROFUTURI LAPIDEM
JECIT DIE XXᴹᴼ MENSIS JUNII A.D. MDCCCLV
HONORATISSIMUS EDWARDUS GALFRIDUS
DERBIENSIS CANCELLARIUS UNIVERSITATIS

Sir Thomas Deane, Thomas N. Deane and Benjamin Woodward
architects built the Oxford Museum, which was founded for
strengthening the study of natural science and in the cause of the
growth of learning. The Right Honourable Edward Geoffrey, Earl
of Derby, Chancellor of the university laid this first stone of a work
destined to benefit posterity on 20 June 1855.

Sir Henry Acland, Baronet, M.D., Professor of Medicine, composed a prayer for the occasion which reflects the controversy over the establishment of such a museum and began thus: 'Grant that the building now to be erected on this spot may foster the progress of those sciences which reveal to us the wonders of thy creative powers.' The drawings chosen for the building after public competition were known as the *Nisi Dominus* design—'Except the Lord build the house, they labour in vain that build it' (Psalm 127.1).

The sectional areas of exhibits were planned as anatomy, geology, mineralogy, palaeontology and zoology, words of Greek derivation.

THE BOTANIC GARDEN

Over the main gateway:

GLORIAE DEI OPT. MAX. HONORI CAROLI REGIS IN USUM
ACAD. ET REIPUB. HENRICUS COMES DANBY D.D. 1632

*To the Glory of God greatest and best and in honour of King
Charles Henry Earl of Danby made this gift for the use of the
university and the community in 1632.*

The Physic Garden, so named until 1840, was like the Bodleian
Library founded for academic and public use. It is the oldest botanical
garden in the country.

Henry Danvers, who was the first and last Earl of Danby, appears
to have had no other connections with Oxford.

The head gardener was once *Horti praefectus*. Each plant has two
Latin names, the first for its *genus* and the second for its *species*.

Optimus Maximus (OPT. MAX.) was a title of Jupiter, taken over to
serve as a title for the Christian God.

Over the entrance door to the west wing
which overlooks the rose garden:

SINE EXPERIENTIA NIHIL SUFFICIENTER SCIRI POTEST

Without experiment it is not possible to know anything adequately.

This inscription has been reset on a modern exterior to the Daubeny
Laboratory (1848), which once served Magdalen for the teaching of
science. The Sherardian professorship of Botany is still attached to
the college.

The rose garden was planted to commemorate the development
of penicillin through research in Oxford in antibiotics and this adds
considerably to the relevance of the inscription, which is attributed
to Roger Bacon (*vide* p. 71).

ALL SOULS COLLEGE

Within the Catte Street entrance lobby above the
doorway into the Codrington Library:

XIᴱ KAL. JUL. MDCCXVI JACTA SUNT FUNDAMENTA
BIBLIOTHECAE CHICHLEIO-CODRINGTONIANAE A
CHRISTOPHERO CODRINGTON ARM. FUNDATAE:
PRAESENTIBUS WILHELMO CODRINGTON ARM. HAEREDE
EX TESTAMENTO, JOHANNE ET WILHELMO CODRINGTON
CHRISTOPHERI CONSANGUINEIS: UNA CUM
BERNARDO GARDINER CUSTODE, SOCIISQUE COLLEGII
QUAMPLURIMIS: PERORANTE EDWARDO YOUNG SOC.

REFECERUNT CODRINGTONIENSES QUAMPLURIMI
A.S. MCMLXXVIII

*On the 21st June 1716 the foundations were laid of the Chichele
Codrington Library established by Christopher Codrington,
Esquire in the presence of William Codrington his heir by will and
testament, John and William Codrington, his kinsmen, together
with Bernard Gardiner the Warden and very many Fellows of the
College, with Edward Young Fellow giving an address.*

*A large number of 'Codringtonians' contributed to the restoration
in 1978.*

This is a replacement foundation stone with an acknowledgement at
the foot to those who contributed towards its cost. On the left of this
addition is the college emblem—the famous mallard, which will by
tradition next be pursued by the Fellows on 14 January 2101.

It has been claimed that this is the largest collegiate room in
Oxford. It is certainly one of the earliest examples of a ground floor
academic library in England.

BALLIOL COLLEGE

In the chapel at the north end of the altar rails:

ὁ δὲ ἀνεξέταστος βίος οὐ βιωτὸς ἀνθρώπῳ

The unexamined life is unliveable for a human being.

This quotation from the Apology (38a) of Socrates by Plato, his younger contemporary, is an appropriate epitaph for the great Platonist, the Revd Professor Benjamin Jowett (1817–1893). It is in minuscule on a light mosaic background above his recumbent effigy on a small wall pedestal monument. Dr Jowett, who had been a Fellow since 1838, was elected Master of Balliol in 1870, when already occupying the Chair of the Regius Professorship of Greek. He held both appointments until his death and served the office of Vice-Chancellor from 1882 to 1886.

These words of Socrates (469–399 BC) came near the end of his defence at his trial in Athens against charges of impiety and the corruption of youth, for which he was sentenced to die by drinking hemlock.

On the south side of the Fisher building
in the Garden quadrangle:

VERBUM NON AMPLIUS   FISHER

A word no more   Fisher

The Revd Henry Fisher (1685–1773) matriculated in 1700 and in 1723 became vicar of Bere Regis in Dorset, where he spent the remainder of his life. This half-hexameter inscription, which he is said to have requested on his death bed, seems to refer to his benefactions to the college, where its translation has for two hundred years been part of Balliol folklore.* Cf. Horace, *Satires* 1.1.121 *Verbum non amplius addam*—'I won't add a word more.'

---

* Peter Howell, 'The Fisher Buildings at Balliol', in the *Balliol College Annual Record* 1981, contains six amusing stanzas about this inscription written for *Balliol Songs* in 1888.

THE KING'S HALL AND
COLLEGE OF BRASENOSE

On a brass tablet in the centre of the screen
at the west end of the Hall:

IN PIAM MEMORIAM WILLELMI HULME DE KEARSLEY IN
AGRO LANCASTRIENSI QUI AMORE IN POPULARES SUOS
PERMOTUS UT JUVENES GRADUM BACALAUREATUS
ADEPTI BONIS STUDIIS DIUTIUS INCUMBERENT ET ALIOS
POSTEA APTIUS DUCERENT MAXIMAM OPUM SUARUM
PARTEM CURATORIBUS COMMISIT — PRESBYTERI IN HOC
COLLEGIO SUB TESTAMENTO ILLIUS ERUDITI ET
MUNIFICENTIA HULMIANA BENEFICATI GRATO IN DEUM
ET IN FUNDATOREM ANIMO HANC TABELLAM P.C.
A.S. MDCCCCII

*To the pious memory of William Hulme of Kearsley in the county
of Lancaster, who moved by good will towards his fellow citizens
committed the major part of his wealth to trustees so that young
men who had gained their bachelor's degree might continue to apply
themselves to their studies and be better fitted to teach others. The
priests educated in this college under the terms of his will and those
placed in benefices by the Hulme trustees undertook the placing of
this tablet in gratitude towards God and the founder. 1902.*

William Hulme (1631–1691) was one of the major benefactors of BNC.
The original endowment was sufficient to provide four exhibitions for
four needy bachelors of arts. With subsequent successful investment
it became possible for a large number of scholarships to be funded
under the trust. The benefactor's name has now been perpetuated
in the appropriate title of the Hulme common room for graduates,
today's successors in the original purpose of the bequest.

In the nineteenth century the Hulme trustees acquired the patronage of many livings, over twenty of them in Cheshire and Lancashire,
where his name is equally well known for educational provision.
William Hulme is buried in the family chapel in Manchester
Cathedral.

CHRIST CHURCH

On the east side of Tom Tower in the Great Quadrangle:

**ANNAE PRINCIPI OPTIMAE SECRETARIUS IPSIUS
PRINCIPALIS ROBERTUS HARLEY HAC IN AEDE POSUIT
QUOD ILLAM COLERET ET HANC AMARET**

*To Anne, the best of Queens, this statue was erected by
Robert Harley, her chief Secretary of State, in this college
to honour her and to express his love for it.*

Below the cornice of the central range of
the Peckwater Quadrangle:

**ATRII PECKWATERIENSIS QUOD SPECTAS LATUS
EXTRUXIT ANTONIUS RADCLIFFE S.T.P. HUJUSCE AEDIS
PRIMO ALUMNUS DEINDE CANONICUS**

*Anthony Radcliffe, Professor of Theology, first a graduate of this
college and then one of its canons, built the side which you see of the
Peckwater Quadrangle.* [He made a major bequest in 1706]

Over the great gateway inside the Canterbury Quadrangle:

**MUNIFICENTIA ALUMNORUM PRAECIPUE
RICARDI ROBINSON ARCHIEP. ARMAGH.**

*Through the generosity of Christ Church men, in particular of
Richard Robinson, Archbishop of Armagh* [c. 1783]

By the entry to Staircase II in the new St Aldate's Quadrangle:

**NOVUM QUOD VIDES ATRIUM MUNIFICENTIA
ALUMNORUM PRAECIPUE H.F. OPPENHEIMER
EXSTRUCTUM EST MCMLXXXVI**

*The new quadrangle which you see was built in 1986 through the
generosity of members, particularly H.F. Oppenheimer.*

24

CHRIST CHURCH
THE CATHEDRAL

On the wall of the west end of the Chapter House and well lit:

THE FOUNDATION STONE OF CARDINAL
WOLSEY'S COLLEGE AT IPSWICH

Above:

LAPIDEM HANC E RUDERIBUS COLLEGII WOLSEIANI
ERUTUM DECANO ET CANONICIS AEDIS CHRISTI
SUPREMO TESTAMENTO LEGAVIT RICARDUS CANNING A.M.
ECCLESIARUM DE HARKSTEAD ET FRISTON
IN AGRO SUFFOLK RECTOR MDCCLXXXIX

Richard Canning, M.A., Rector of Harkstead and Friston in Suffolk, left
by his last will and testament in 1789 to the Dean and Chapter of Christ
Church this stone which was rescued from the ruins of Wolsey's college.

The following words can be deciphered from the foundation stone,
which had presumably lain among the ruins for over two centuries.
It is therefore remarkable that it is still in reasonable condition apart
from the loss of a section at the top, which can be reconstructed.
The spelling is unusual and the sentence construction strange, but
the meaning is apparent.

ANO CH[RIS]TI MDXX[V]III ET REGNI HENRICI OCTAVI
REGIS ANGLIAE XX MENSIS VERO JUNII XV POSITUM P
JOHEN EPM LIDEN (LIDENSEM)

In the year of Christ 152[8] and the twentieth of the reign of Henry
VIII King of England, this stone was placed by John, Bishop of
Lydda, on the fifteenth day of the month of June.

Thomas Wolsey (1475–1530) was born at Ipswich and studied at
Magdalen, where he became Fellow in 1497 and for a short while
Master of Magdalen College School. In 1525 he set in hand the
establishment of Cardinal College and three years later in imitation
of the dual foundation a century and a half before of Winchester
College and New College by William of Wykeham embarked on a

similar policy in his native town. Both attempts were discontinued after his fall from power in 1529 and it seems doubtful whether the institution at Ipswich was ever effectively begun.

John Holte was a suffragan Bishop of London, on whom was conferred the courtesy title of Bishop of Lydda *in partibus* (from another part of Christendom).

In the north cloister walk of the former Augustinian priory:

PERPETUA ESTO

INTER HOS PARIETES

MEMORIA

OTHO NICHOLSON ARM.

QUI

URBEM HANC HINXEIANIS AQUIS IRRIGAVIT

PRISTINAM HUJUS AEDIS BIBLIOTHECAM

VETUSTATE COLLAPSAM

INSTAURAVIT, INSTRUXIT

BENEFACTOR EXIMIUS A.D. MDCXIII

Everlasting be the memory within these walls of Otho Nicholson Esquire, who supplied this city with water from Hinksey and restored and refitted the original library of this college which had fallen into ruin with age. An outstanding benefactor. 1613.

His initials O.N. decorate the magnificent conduit erected at Carfax in 1610, which to ease the traffic problems of the period was transferred to Nuneham Park in 1789.

The other reference is to the Old Library (until 1772) of the college on the top floor of the original *Frater* of the monastery. The space now houses the library which Richard Allestree left in 1681 for the use of his successors in the Chair of the Regius Professor of Divinity.

The two opening words of this memorial were those frequently on the lips of Paolo Sarpi, a contemporary ecclesiastical historian speaking about his native Venice.

An epitaph in a scrolled frame beneath a painted bust on one of the piers in the eastern aisle of the north transept:

PAUCIS NOTUS PAUCIORIBUS IGNOTUS
HIC JACET
DEMOCRITUS JUNIOR
CUI VITAM DEDIT ET MORTEM
MELANCHOLIA
OBIIT VIII ID. JAN AC MDCXXXIX

Known to a few men, quite unknown to even fewer, here lies Democritus Junior, for whom melancholy provided life and death. He died on 6 January in the year of Christ 1639.

Robert Burton, born in 1577, was in 1599 elected a Student of Christ Church, where he spent the rest of his life, and was presented in 1616 by the college to the living of St Thomas in Oxford. He adopted the pseudonym of 'Democritus Junior' for the publication of *The Anatomy of Melancholy* in 1621, a compendium about the disease, with quotations from classical and medieval and renaissance authors and including superstitious theories. In contrast Democritus, who lived in northern Greece in the fifth century BC, was known as the 'laughing philosopher', amused by the follies of men.

It seems likely that Robert Burton composed his own anonymous epitaph. He makes the point that although few people knew him, his work was known to many. It certainly makes interesting reading today. He did not record that he left his books to the college, of which he was librarian when the Old Library now so named was restored (see opposite).

The last line is only comprehensible with the stop placed after ID. (Idus) to indicate that it is an abbreviation.*

---

* *Vide* note on Roman chronology, p. 75.

On the second pillar on the north side of the nave:

JOHANNI WALRONDO
ADOLESCENTI SINGULARI INDOLE, PIETATE, MORIBUS
SUAVISSIMIS, LITERATURA EXCULTISSIMO, NATO BOVII
DEVON, INSTITUTO WESTMON. IN HAC AEDE
PER BIENNIUM MAXIMO CUM PROFECTU
VERSATO AC IBIDEM PIE DEFUNCTO,
DILECTISSIMO FILIO ET HAEREDI
JOHANNES WALRONDUS DE BOVY
ARMIGER DEVON. CUM JANA
UXORE, MEMORIAE AC SUMMI
AMORIS ERGO
POSUIT

SI MEA CUM MATRIS VALUISSENT VOTA DEDISSES
FUNUS IDEM NOBIS QUOD TIBI NATE DAMUS
SED QUONIAM NOSTRIS VOTIS DEUS OBSTITIT AEQUUS
ANTE MEA, ET MATRIS FUNERA, FUNUS HABE.
OBIIT JUNII 25, 1602
AETAT. 17.

TEMPORA QUAE VITAE DEERANT, SINT ADDITA FAMAE:
AURO QUI DIGNUS, VIVAT IN AERE RUDI.

BEATI MORTUI, QUI IN DOMINO MORIUNTUR

*For John Walrond, a young man of singular talents and piety and
pleasing character, highly educated in literature, born at Bovey in
Devon, educated at Westminster, who passed two years in this
college making very great progress and died here piously, their
beloved son and heir. John Walrond of Bovey with Jane his wife
set up this [monument] in memory and in great love.*

*If my prayers with those of your mother had been answered,
you would have given us the same last rites as we are giving to you,
my son. But since a just God did not grant our requests, receive
these last honours before I have mine and your mother hers.
He died on 25 June 1602 at the age of seventeen.*

*Let the years that were taken from his life be added to
his reputation. May he who was worthy of gold live on
in homely bronze.*

Blessed are the dead who die in the Lord. (Revelation 14.13)

This brass was carefully conserved in 1988. It had been covered in
grey paint and brown varnish and bolted to the wall. Repair and
repainting revealed a portrait of a young man kneeling in prayer with
a scroll issuing from his mouth—*Credo quod redemptor meus vivit*—'I
believe that my Redeemer liveth' (Job 19.25).The brass is surrounded
by painted strapwork with shields of arms and inscriptions above
and beneath. At the lower corners the dates A.D. 1602 and Aug 9 or
Aug 31 show the speed with which this monument was erected. One
mystery remains. The ugly iron rivets may have been driven into the
stone to secure the brass against robbers, but other holes were found
indicating that there may once have been a door or protective grille in
front of a recess in the Norman pillar. It has been suggested that this
might originally have been made to serve as a niche for a small statue.

Other memorial brasses on the walls of the cathedral, which
were corroded, and Victorian brasses on the floor have received
similar protective treatment, for which the Friends of Christ Church
Cathedral were able to provide some of the necessary funds.

On a monument against the west wall of the south transept:

M.S. HEIC JACET EDOARDUS LITTLETON, BARO DE
MOUNSLOWE, IN ACRO SALOPIENSI; MAGNI SIGILLI
ANGLIAE CUSTOS; EDR̄I LITTLETON DE HENLEY IN EODEM
EQUITIS FIL: NAT: MAX: ORIUNDUS ILLE EX ANTIQUA
PROSAPIA THOMAE LITTLETON EQUITIS DE BALNEO, QUI
SUB EDR̄O IV^TO JUSTICIARIUS, LEGES ANGL: MUNICIPALES
(PRIUS INDIGESTAS) IN ENCHEIRIDION FAELICITER
REDUXIT: OPUS IN OMNE AEVUM IC^TIS VENERANDUM.
EDOARDI NOSTRI (AVORUM NOMINE NON MINORIS)
EDUCATIO AEDE[M] HANC REGIAM NON MEDIOCRITER
ORNAVIT. AB HINC AD INTER[IUS] TEMPLUM LONDINI A
VOCATUS, NULLUM HONORIS FASTIGIUM NON MERUIT,
NON ATTIGIT: IN SENATU, IN FORO MERITISSIME
SPECTABILIS: PARTIBUS CAROLI MARTYRIS BEATI,
FLAGRANTE CIVILI PERDUELLIUM RABIE, TOTUS
ADHAESIT; ET IN EXECRANDA CIVITATIS HUJUS
OBSIDIONE, STRENUUS REGIAE MAJESTATIS ASSERTOR,
CHILIARCHA SAGUM INDUIT, TAM MARTI IDONEUS QUAM
MERCURIO. UBI JUVENIS PRODIGIOSA JECIT FUTURAE
GLORIAE FUNDAMENTA, HIC TANDEM AETATE PROVECTA
INTER ARMORUM STREPITUS GENEROSAM EXHALAVIT
ANIMAM, ANNO A CHRISTO MDCXLV, DISERTISSIMO
OPTIMOQUE VIRO DOCTORE HAMMOND UNIVERSITATIS
OXONIENSIS ORATORE PUBL: AD EXEQUIAS PERORANTE.

ANNA LITTLETON UNICA FILIA ET HAERES; THOMAE
LITTLETON BARONETTI VIDUA MONUMENTUM HOC
RELLIGIOSE PONI CURAVIT MDCLXXXIII

Sacred to his memory. Here lies Edward Littleton, Baron of Mountslowe,
in the County of Shropshire, keeper of the Great Seal of England, eldest
son of Sir Edward Littleton of Henley in the same county. He was sprung
from the ancient line of Thomas Littleton, Knight of the Bath, who, under
Edward IV, was a judge who successfully codified the municipal laws of
England (which hitherto had never been edited) in a handbook—a work to
be revered for the whole era of Jesus Christ. To return to our Edward
Littleton (who was not inferior to the fame of his forbears)—his education
brought no little honour to this royal College. From here he was called to
the Inner Temple, where he both earned and gained all the highest
distinctions. In Parliament and at the Bar he was most deservedly
respected. When madness and treason of Civil War broke out, he clung
wholly to the cause of the blessed martyr Charles I. In the abominable siege
of this city he was an energetic champion of the king's authority, and
assumed the military cloak as commander of a thousand soldiers, as suited
to Mars as once he was to Mercury. Where as a young man he had laid the
foundations that foreshadowed his glory to come, here at last, growing old
he breathed out his noble soul amid the clash of arms, in the year of our
Lord 1645. That most eloquent and excellent man, Doctor Hammond,
Public Orator of the University of Oxford, pronounced the funeral oration.

Anne Littleton his only daughter and heir, widow of Thomas Littleton,
Baronet, in due devotion, had this memorial set up 1683.

There are here, besides an interesting variety of lettering, some
archaic forms of spelling and other peculiarities. Close inspection
of the monument will reveal attempts of an unlettered stonecutter at emendation—TIS was added to IC. If expansion to JESUS
CHRISTI was intended a further error crept in with a wrong form of
genitive case. Missing letters have here been added to AEDE[M] and
INTER[IUS], beneath which an s had been incised. One mistake was
overlooked—JUVEMS, which has been corrected to JUVENIS.

In St Lucy's chapel, the tablet nearest to the sacristy steps:

P.M.S.

HOC LOCO IN SPEM

FUTURI SAECULI DEPOSITUM JACET

JOHANNIS BANKES

QUI REGINALIS COLLECII IN HAC ACADEMIA

ALUMNUS

EQUES AURATUS ORNATISSIMUS

ATTORNATUS GENERALIS

DE COMMUNI BANCO CAP. JUSTICIARIUS

A SECRETIORIBUS CONSILIIS REGI CAROLO,

PERITIAM, INTEGRITATEM, FIDEM

EGREGIE PRAESTITIT

EX AEDE CHRISTI, IN AEDES CHRISTI*

TRANSIIT MENSE DECEMBRIS DIE 28

ANNO DOMINI 1644

AETATIS SUAE 55

NON NOBIS DÑE NON NOBIS

SED NOMINI TUO SIT GLORIA

Sacred to his pious memory in the hope of life to come lie the remains of John Bankes, who was an undergraduate of The Queen's College in this university, a most distinguished knight, Attorney General, Lord Chief Justice of the Common Bench, and a member of the Privy Council of King Charles. He possessed skill, integrity and loyalty in a high degree. He went from Christ Church to Christ's House on 28 December in the Year of Our Lord 1644 at the age of 55.

Not unto us, O Lord, not unto us, but to thy name let there be glory.
(Psalm 115.1)

Sir John Bankes (1589–1644) accompanied the King to Oxford. He received the Honorary Degree of Doctor of Civil Law from the university on 20 December 1642. Lady Bankes was at the time occupied with the heroic defence of their home, Corfe Castle, against the Parliamentarians.

---

* *Ex Aede Christi* (the 'House') and *in Aedes Christi* together create a pun.

On the last pillar in the south aisle of the nave:

EDOARDUS POCOCK S.T.D.
(CUJUS SI NOMEN AUDIAS,
NIHIL HIC DE FAMA DESIDERES)
NATUS EST OXONIAE NOV. 8, A.D. 1604
SOCIUS IN COLLEGIUM CORPORIS CHRISTI
COOPTATUS 1628
IN LINGUAE ARABICAE LECTURAM PUBLICE
HABENDAM PRIMUS EST INSTITUTUS 1636
DEINDE ETIAM IN HEBRAICAM PROFESSORI
REGIO SUCCESSIT 1648
DESIDERATISSIMO MARITO SEPT 10 1691
IN CAELUM REVERSO
MARIA BURDET
EX QUA NOVENAM SUSCEPIT SOBOLEM
TUMULUM HUNC MAERENS POSUIT

Edward Pocock, Doctor of Divinity (should you hear his name spoken
you would not need to be told here of his reputation) was born in Oxford on
8 Nov 1604, and became a Fellow of Corpus Christi in 1628. He was the
first to be appointed to the public lectureship in Arabic in 1636 and then to a
lectureship in Hebrew, succeeding as Regius Professor of Hebrew in 1648.
When he returned to heaven on 10 September 1691 Mary Burdet, by
whom he had nine children, mourned her loss and erected this monument.

William Laud (1573–1645) established a chair of Arabic in Christ
Church when he was Chancellor of the university. He would, when
President of St John's College, have known Edward Pocock as a
promising young scholar of oriental languages. Since 1937 the Laudian
Professorship of Arabic has been attached to St John's.

The first five Regius Professorships of Divinity, Civil Law, Medicine, Hebrew and Greek were founded by King Henry VIII in 1546
and associated with Christ Church. Memorials of other holders of
these chairs will be found in the cathedral.

On the south wall of the ante-chapel, to which it was transferred from the Latin chapel when the cathedral was extended in 1872:

M.S.

JOHANNES FELL, S.T.D. LONGWORTHIAE BERCHERIENSIUM
NATUS, IN HANC AEDEM A DECANO PATRE ADMISSUS
ALUMNUS UNDECENNIS, MAGISTRALEM TOGAM ANTE INDUIT
QUAM SUMERET VIRILEM, SACROS ORDINES DIACONATUS,
VACILLANTE ECCLESIA PRESBYTERATUS, PENITUS EVERSA,
AUSUS EST SUSCIPERE. ET ECCLESIAE RELIQUIAS EA FOVIT
CURA QUAE PRAELUSISSE VIDEATUR EPISCOPATUI. SPECTATA
IN UTRUMQUE CAROLUM FIDE, A FILIO TANDEM RESTAURATO
TUTELAM HUJUS ECCLESIAE DECANUS ACCEPIT, ET HUIC
TANTAE PLUSQUAM PAR PROVINCIAE, EPISCOPATUM UNA
OXONIENSEM FAELICITER ADMINISTRAVIT. SED DUM SALUTI
PUBLICAE INTENTUS NEGLIGERET SUAM, AB ECCLESIA ITERUM
PERICLITANTE DESIDERATUS EST.

NATUS JUN. 23, A.D. 1625   DIACONUS A.D. 1647
PRESBYTER A.D. 1649   DECANUS A.D. 1660
EPISCOPUS A.D. 1675   MORTUUS JULIO A.D. 1686

MONUMENTUM SIBI FIERI VETUIT BEATISSIMUS PATER
POSUERE THOMAS WILLIS ET HENRICUS JONES E DUABUS
SORORIBUS NEPOTES, PIETATIS ESSE ARBITRATI HUIC UNI
EJUS MANDATO NON OBTEMPERARE. PRAEDICANDUM SIBI
MINIME CENSUERE HUNC TALEM VIRUM; MELIOREM QUAM
UT VELLET LAUDARI, MAJOREM QUAM UT POSSET.
DESIDERATISSIMI PATRIS PIETATEM,
NON HOC SAXUM SED HAEC TESTENTUR MOENIA:
MUNIFICENTIAM HUJUS LOCI AEDIFICIA;
LIBERALITATEM ALUMNI;
QUID IN MORIBUS INFORMANDIS POTUIT, HAEC AEDES;
QUID IN PUBLICIS CURIS SUSTENTANDIS, ACADEMIA;
QUID IN PROPAGANDA RELIGIONE, ECCLESIA;
QUAM FELICITER JUVENTUTEM ERUDIERIT, PROCERUM FAMILIAE;
QUAM PRAECLARE DE REPUBLICA MERUERIT, TOTA ANGLIA;
QUANTUM DE BONIS LITERIS, UNIVERSUS ORBIS LITERATUS.

Sacred to his memory, John Fell, Doctor of Divinity, born at Longworth in Berkshire, admitted to Christ Church by the Dean, his father, as an undergraduate at the age of eleven. He put on the Master's gown before he wore that of manhood. He had the courage to take on the holy orders of a deacon, when the Church of England was tottering, and those of a priest when it was completely overthrown. He nursed what remained of the Church with a care such as seemed to foreshadow the office of Bishop. Of proven loyalty to both Charles I and Charles II, he received at the hands of the latter, on his restoration, the guardianship of Christ Church as Dean. And, being more than capable even of that great office, he successfully held the see of Oxford along with it. But in devoting himself to the public good, he neglected his own, and the Church lost him just as it came into danger once again.

Born 23 June 1625   Deacon 1647   Priest 1649   Dean 1660
Bishop 1675   Died 10 July 1686

The most blessed of Fathers forbade any memorial for himself. This was set up by Thomas Willis and Henry Jones, his nephews and sons of his two sisters, thinking it a matter of duty to disobey him in this one instruction of his. They thought it wrong to leave to their own commendation a man of such quality, too good to wish, too great to be able to be praised. To the piety of this most mourned of Fathers let not this stone but these walls bear witness: to his munificence, the buildings of this place; to his generosity, his pupils; to his ability as a trainer in character, this college; as a bearer of public responsibilities, this university; as a diffuser of religion, the Church; to his success as an educator of youth, the families of the nobility; to his glorious services to the state, all England; to his services to letters, the whole world of letters.

Samuel Fell was Dean of Christ Church 1638–48. He entertained King Charles I when Oxford was the Royalist capital, and was subsequently ejected from office. At the restoration of the monarchy in 1660 his son John Fell became Dean and subsequently Bishop of Oxford. He made a major contribution in the completion of Wolsey's Great Quadrangle and later the tower by Christopher Wren. Though Christ Church might regard him almost as a second founder he was not so popular in the university, of which he was Vice-Chancellor 1666–69.

On the third pillar on the north side of the nave:

GRAVISSIMO PRAESULI
GEORGIO EPISCOPO CLONENSI
VIRO
SEU INGENII ET ERUDITIONIS LAUDEM
SEU PROBITATIS ET BENEFICIENTIAE SPECTEMUS
INTER PRIMOS OMNIUM AETATUM NUMERANDO.
SI CHRISTIANUS FUERIS
SI AMANS PATRIAE
UTROQUE NOMINE GLORIARI POTES
BERKLEIUM VIXISSE.
OBIIT ANNUM AGENS SEPTUAGESIMUM TERTIUM
NATUS ANNO CHRISTI MDCLXXIX
ANNA CONJUX
L.M.P.*

*To the most respected prelate, George, Bishop of Cloyne, a man who,
whether we consider the praise of his intellect and learning or that of
his integrity and beneficence, must be counted among the first men of
all ages. If you area Christian or a lover of your country,
on both accounts you can be proud that Berkeley lived.
He was born in the year of Christ 1679
and died in his seventy-third year.
Anne his mourning wife set this up in glad recognition of his desert.*

The great philosopher and Anglican bishop, who held the see of
Cloyne near Cork from 1734 to 1752, died a year after coming to
Oxford, where his son was a Christ Church undergraduate at the
time, and he was given burial in the Cathedral. A floor slab in front
of the monument carries an epitaph by Alexander Pope: 'To Berkeley
every virtue under heaven' (*Epilogue to Satires* 11.78).

---

* The abbreviation L.M.P. is open to several interpretations, among them *libens* (glad) or
lugens (mourning) and *moerens* (mourning) or *merito* (in recompense). The above translation
is a combination of these alternatives.

On a roundel encircling his profile bust next to the pulpit:

HENRICUS ALDRICH S.T.P. AEDIS CHRISTI DECANUS ET
GRANDE TOTIUS ACADEMIAE ORNAMENTUM

And beneath:

VIXIT VIR CLARISSIMUS ANNIS LXIII
OB. XIX KAL. JAN. MDCCX

NE CINERES DEFUNCTI SINE NOMINE ET TITULO DIUTIUS
NEGLECTI JACERENT GEO. CLARKE QUI VIVUM COLUIT ET
AMAVIT AM. B.M. FECIT A.D. MDCCXXXII

*Henry Aldrich, Doctor of Divinity, Dean of Christ Church
and great ornament of the whole university.*

*This most distinguished man lived for 63 years
and died on 14 December 1710.*

*George Clarke, who respected and loved him during life, placed this
tribute to his deserving memory so that the ashes of the dead man
might no longer remain nameless and without inscription. 1732.*

Henry Aldrich (1647–1710) was Dean of Christ Church from 1689
until his death. In addition to the demands of this double role he
served as Vice-Chancellor from 1692 to 1695. He was a talented
musician and skilled amateur architect, who designed All Saints
Church (which now provides a library for Lincoln College) and a
new quadrangle for Christ Church to replace the old Peckwater Inn.

George Clarke (1661–1736), Fellow of All Souls from 1680 until his
death, was a lawyer and the Burgess for the university from 1717 to
1736, and was equally distinguished as an architect. He was responsible
for the design of the new library for Christ Church which completed
the Peckwater Quadrangle. His own wall-monument and epitaph is
on the south wall of the ante-chapel of All Souls College.

A brass plaque to the right of the south
door leading into the cloister:

HANC CATHEDRAM EFFICIE DESIDERATISSIMI
IN X̄T̄O PATRIS SAMUELIS WILBERFORCE ORNATAM,
IN MEMORIAM EPISCOPATUS PER ANNOS FERE XXV
EGREGIE GESTI,
PER QUOD TEMPUS
TRES COMITATUS E TOTIDEM DIOECESIBUS
IN UNAM CONSTITUTOS
TANTA SAGACITATE, INGENIO TAM VERSATILI
TAMQUE SUAVI,
DILIGENTIA TAM INDEFESSA SIBI DEVINXIT,
UT CONCORDIA INTER OMNES FACILE COALUERIT,
PONENDAM CURAVERUNT ISTIUS DIOECESEOS
CLERUS FIDELESQUE
A.D. MDCCCLXXVI

*The clergy and the laity of this diocese commissioned the making of
this throne crowned with the portrait head of their greatly missed
Father in Christ, Samuel Wilberforce, to remember his outstanding
episcopate of almost twenty-five years. During this period he united
in his charge three counties brought into one from three dioceses,
with such practical wisdom, with a mind so adaptable and so
agreeable, with efforts so tireless, that harmony was easily
established between all parties. 1876.*

Bishop Wilberforce (1805–1873) held the see of Oxford from 1845 to
1870, when an episcopal throne was set in position as his memorial.
Of this only the portrait head now set over the door into the cloisters
remains. In 1937 it was decided to replace the Victorian throne with a
cathedra (seat) placed on the other side of the chancel, over which the
present canopy was placed in 1967. This was done to allow access to
the chancel from the Military Chapel. Berkshire was included in the
Oxford diocese in 1836 and Buckinghamshire in 1845.

In the centre of a ledger in the nave:

EDWARD BOUVERIE PUSEY S.T.P. LINGUAE HEBRAICAE
PROFESSORIS ET HUJUSCE AEDIS CANONICI QUI IN PACE
ET MISERICORDIA JESU OBDORMIVIT D. SEP XVI
MDCCCLXXXII NAT. ANNOS LXXXII DIES XXIV

BENEDICTUS DEUS QUI NON AMOVIT ORATIONEM MEAM
ET MISERICORDIAM SUAM A ME

To Edward Bouverie Pusey, Doctor of Divinity, Regius Professor of
Hebrew and Canon of this Cathedral who fell asleep in the peace and
mercy of Jesus on 16 September 1882 aged 82 years and 24 days.

Blessed be God who has not turned away my prayer
nor his mercy from me. (Psalm 66.20)

The Revd Dr E.B. Pusey (1800–1882), educated at Eton and Christ
Church, was made a Fellow of Oriel in 1822 where he began an
association with John Keble (1792–1866) and John Henry Newman
(1801–1890) and thereby was one of the leaders of the Oxford Movement whose supporters became known as Puseyites or Tractarians.
He returned to Christ Church in 1828 where he spent the remaining
fifty-four years of his life as an Anglo-Catholic opponent of reform
in the Church and in university institutions.

This is the second memorial on a large slab which contains
epitaphs to his wife and to two of his daughters. The first is to Maria
Catherine who died in 1841 at the age of 30 in the eleventh year of
their marriage. After his own memorial was added below hers there
are tributes to his eldest daughter Catherine, who died aged 14 in
1844, and to a second daughter Lucy, who died in infancy in 1832. An
inscription on a tomb in the cathedral garth records the death of his
only son, Philip in 1880, at the age of 49. All these memorials must
have been placed by his surviving daughter.

Pusey House began in 1884 as a 'memorial library' and place 'of
sacred learning'. Its motto is *Deus scientiarum Dominus*—'The Lord is
a God of knowledge' (I Samuel 2.3).

CORPUS CHRISTI COLLEGE

On the cylinder of the Pelican Sundial:

CARMINA IN IMA BASI HOROLOGII
SCRIPTA SUBTER CYLINDRUM

Verses written at the very base of the sundial under the cylinder.

ASPICE PERPETUO LABENTIA SYDERA CURSU,
ALTERNIS VICIBUS LUMEN AC UMBRA REGUNT.
LUMEN AC UMBRA REGUNT NEBULIS RECIDENTIBUS ASTRIS,
FINES CURRICULI NOVIT UTRUMQUE SUI.
TUQUE REGIS, FACILEMQUE VIAM VENIENTIBUS OFFERS
CUNCTAQUE CONSUETIS, ALMA COLUMNA, MODIS.
SUNT IN TE SPECIES, SUNT COELI SIGNA SERENI
ACCEDANT CAPITI LUMINA, PHOEBUS ERIS.
NAMQUE DOCES PARITER, PHOEBES PHOEBIQUE LABORES
TEMPORA, QUISQUE DIES, MENSIS AC ANNUS ERIT.
AUREUS HIC NUMERUS, SOLIS CYCLUSQUE PERENNIS;
CUNCTA CALENDARIUM QUAE DOCET, ISTA DOCET.
ASTRORUM ASPECTUS, MEDIOS HIC CONSPICE MOTUS,
NEC LATET IGNOTIS CYNTHIA BLANDA LOCIS.
DANTUR INAEQUALES, FINESQUE AEQUAUBUS HORIS,
PHOEBE DAS NOCTU. TU QUOQUE PHOEBE DIE.

See the stars gliding in their eternal course, light or shadow is master as its turn comes round. Light or shadow is master as the clouds cross the stars; each one of them knows how far to run his course. You too, column of our college, in your accustomed way, are mistress of them all and give them an early path as they arrive. In you is the beauty, in you the signs of the peaceful heavens; let the luminaries consent to your leadership, and you will be the sun himself. For you tell not only of the toils of moon and sun, but of the seasons, and what day, what month, and what year it will be. See the golden number, and here the perpetual cycle of the sun: everything in the calendar is shown by this column. Here are the aspects of the stars [planets], here see their mean periods, and enchanting Cynthia, goddess of the moon, does not have to hide away unheralded. The unequal hours are shown, as are the limits of the equal ones: the moon shows them by night, and by day the sun.

On the cornice above the prism of the Sundial:

POSUI DEUM ADJUTOREM NOSTRUM
EST REPOSITA JUSTITIAE CORONA
GRATIA DEI MECUM
1581 EST DEO GRATIA

I have made God my helper.
A crown is set on justice.
The grace of God be with me.
1581 Here is thanks to God.

At the foot on the north side:

HORAS OMNES COMPLECTOR

I embrace all hours.

The sundial was erected by Charles Turnbull, a Fellow of the college in 1581, who provided an eclipse table for the years 1581 to 1597 and renewed it for the years 1605–1619. A new set of 24 diagrams was then added for 1625–1646, which has been used for the present re-painting.

The sundial was restored in 1976 under the direction of Dr Philip Pattenden, a former scholar of the college.*

Est deo gratia is the motto of Richard Foxe (*c.* 1448–1528) the founder in 1517 when he was Bishop of Winchester. These words have been incorporated in a frieze on a building erected in 1885 on the opposite side of Merton Street.

IN DOMINO CONFIDO	SIT LAUS DEO	EST DEO GRACIA
I trust in the Lord	*Let there be praise to God*	*Thanks to God*

---

* He has fully documented its history in *Sundials at an Oxford College* (1979), from which the above information and translations are with his generous permission reproduced.

In the cloister on the south wall—the third inscription
to the left of the entrance:

IN MEMORIAM
RICARDI WINN LIVINGSTONE
EQUITIS AURATI
SOCII MCMIV—MCMXXIV
PRAESIDIS MCMXXXIII—MCML
OBIIT DIE XXVI DECEMBRI MCMLX
ANNO AETATIS SUAE LXXX

GRAECITATIS LIBERALITATIS HUMANITATIS
ANTISTES PROPUGNATOR EXEMPLAR
ERUDIENDAE JUVENTUTI OPERAM DEDIT
NOTOS IGNOTOS COMITER EXCEPIT
SUAVILOQUENTI FUIT SERMONE
PRISCA MORUM ELEGANTIA

In memory of Sir Richard Winn Livingstone,
Fellow from 1904 to 1924 and President from 1933 to 1950.
He died on 26 December 1960 in the eightieth year of his life.

Exponent, champion and model of Greek learning, of liberality
and humanity, he applied himself to the education of youth.
He gave a kind welcome to friend and stranger alike.
He was of pleasant speech in conversation and
of old-fashioned elegance in manners.

An example of the ideal Oxford tutor whom the governing body
welcomed back as President of his college after a nine-year absence
as Vice-Chancellor of the Queen's University of Belfast. He was
Vice-Chancellor of Oxford University from 1944 to 1947.

JESUS COLLEGE

A bronze plaque inside the gatehouse
above the window of the porter's lodge:

MCMVII—MCMX
HIC TRIENNIUM TRANSEGIT
THOMAS EDWARDUS LAWRENCE
ARABIAE JACENTIS VINDEX IMPAVIDUS
CUJUS NOMEN NE OBSOLESCERET
POSUIT HOC AES COLLEGII JESU JUVENTUS

SAPIENTIA AEDIFICAVIT SIBI DOMUM
EXCIDIT COLUMNAS SEPTEM

1907—1910
Thomas Edward Lawrence,
the fearless champion of oppressed Arabia,
spent three years here.
The Junior Common Room of Jesus College placed this brass
so that his name should not be forgotten.

Wisdom has built her house, she has hewn her seven pillars.
(Proverbs, 9.1)

Thomas Edward Lawrence (1888–1935) was born in Oxford and educated at the City of Oxford High School, then in George Street. A memorial plaque has been affixed to the family home at 2 Polstead Road where the summer house he used in the garden is still occupied. In 1919 he was given a Fellowship at All Souls for the purpose of writing *The Seven Pillars of Wisdom*, his narrative of his experiences in the desert published in 1926. The title was taken from the Old Testament quotation at the foot of the memorial, which was provided by the undergraduates at Jesus in 1936, the year after Lawrence's sudden death.

KEBLE COLLEGE

In the chapel cloister:

MEMENTOTE* ALUMNORUM FAMULORUMQUE
HUJUS COLLEGII QUI VINDICES LIBERTATIS PRODIGI VITAE
PRO PATRIA ANIMAS REDDIDERUNT
MCMXIV–MCMXIX

*Be mindful of the graduates and the members of staff of this college
who in defence of freedom and in disregard of life sacrificed
themselves for their country. 1914–1919.*

And at some distance, in Little Clarendon Street on its south side
at the Jericho end, on a small cast-iron plaque in a service entry:

HOC IN LOCO IRENE FRUDE
COLLEGII KEBLENSIS ALUMNORUM BENIGNISSIMA ALTRIX
INGENTISSIMA JENTACULA
XXXV FERME PER ANNOS COTIDIE SUPPEDITAVIT
CUJUS REI BENE MEMORES EIDEM ALUMNI
HOC MONUMENTUM FACIENDUM CURAVERUNT
A.D. IV KAL. NOV. MCMLXXVI

*On this site Irene Frude, the most kindly landlady of
undergraduates of Keble College, provided each day for almost
thirty-five years enormous breakfasts. Some with fond memories of
this undertook the placing of this tribute to her on 9 October 1976.*

This must be the only Latin inscription about a keeper of licensed
lodgings, a feature of Oxford life now extinct.

The site of the housing at this end of Little Clarendon Street was
redeveloped to provide university accommodation on the north side
of Wellington Square.

---

* *Mementote* is the plural form of the imperative of the verb *meminisse*, to remember. Cf.
memento in its singular form.

KELLOGG COLLEGE

On the west wall of the central courtyard:

AEDES REWLEIANAS CONVERTIT
CONVERSAS IMMO ET TRANSFORMAVIT
TOTO CUM VICO MUNIFICENTIA
SOCIETATIS W.K. KELLOGG BIS EXPERTA
LARGITER ANNO DOMINI MCMLXIII
POST LUSTRA* IV MAGNIFICENTER
CONSULIT UT SENIORES BONIS LITERIS ARTIBUS
FRUI POSSENT STUDIAQUE BENE INCEPTA
AD USUM PERFICERENTUR

*The munificence of the W.K. Kellogg Foundation converted,
or rather converted and transformed, Rewley House, together with
the whole neighbourhood. Generously in 1963, magnificently
twenty years later, it sought to provide that older people should
be able to enjoy literature and arts and that studies well begun
should be brought to profitable ends.*

The name of Rewley Abbey, a Cistercian monastery on a site just
to the east of the present railway station, has been preserved in a
building in Wellington Square once used as a girls' school which
was transferred from a former Rewley House in Gloucester Green.
This was acquired by the university in 1926 for the establishment of a
centre for the work of a delegacy for Extra-Mural Studies. In 1964 the
Department for Continuing Education was set up with the financial
support described in the inscription. A further dimension in the work
of this department was made possible with the establishment of the
Kellogg Residential Centre.

Rewley House became the thirty-sixth collegiate foundation of the
university in 1990 as the base for part-time degree courses in Oxford,
and its name was changed to Kellogg College in 1994.

---

* *Vide* p. 75 for an explanation of *lustra*.

MAGDALEN COLLEGE

On the west wall to the left of the small doorway
immediately after entering the ante-chapel:

ALLELUIA
GLORIA IN EXCELSIS DEO
IN PIAM MEMORIAM JOHANNIS STAINER
A.M. MUS. DOC., COLL. HUJUSCE NECNON ECCL. CATH.
S. PAULI APUD LONDINIENSES ORGANISTAE MUSICES
IN UNIVERSITATE OXONIENSI PROFESSORIS.
VIRI LEPIDI SCITI DULCIS DOCTI QUI ARTEM SI QUA
ALIA CAELESTEM SEU MELODIAS COMPONEBAT SIVE
ORGANA PULSANDO REDDEBAT NUNQUAM NON SANCTE
TRACTAVIT IN CHRISTO OBDORMIVIT VERONAE
PRID KAL. APRIL A.S. MCMI AETAT LXI

HOC MARMOR POSUIT CONJUGIS AMOR

*Hallelujah, glory to God in the highest. To the pious memory of John
Stainer, Master of Arts, Doctor of Music, organist of this college and of
St Paul's Cathedral in London, Professor of Music in the University of
Oxford. A man of agreeable nature, wise, gentle and learned, who never
failed to use in holiness that art which is heavenly above all others,
whether he was composing melodies or rendering them by playing the
organ. He fell asleep in Christ at Verona on 31 March 1901 aged 61.*

His loving wife set up this marble tablet.

Sir John Stainer (1840–1901) was knighted in 1888 for his contribution
to music, which had also included service as one of Her Majesty's
Inspectors of Schools with national responsibility for the subject. In
the previous year he had composed the well-known oratorio *The
Crucifixion*. He became the Heather Professor of Music at Oxford and
was made an Honorary Fellow of Magdalen in 1889. His grave is in
Holywell Cemetery and there is a memorial window in the Church
of St Cross.

MERTON COLLEGE

In the ante-chapel to the left of the great west window:

M.S.

HENRICUS SAVILE, MILES,

COLEGII { MERTONENSIS CUSTOS
ETONENSIS PRAPOSITUS

FUI

EXUVIAS CORPORIS FRUSTRA SIT QUI HIC QUAERAT

SERVAT PRAENOBILE DEPOSITUM ETONA

PERENNEM VIRTUTUM AC BENEFACTORUM MEMORIAM

QUIBUS COLLEGIUM UTRUMQUE, ACADEMIAM INPRIMIS

OXONIENSEM COMPLEXUS EST, IPSUMQUE ADEO

MUNDUM HABET SIBI DEBENDI REUM,

AFFECTUS INSUPER PIENTISSIMAE UXORIS

POSSIDET ISTE LAPIS

B.M.P. MARGARETA CONJUX OBSEQUENTISSIMA

IN HOC UNO QUOD POSUIT PIE IMMORIGERA

OBIIT ANNO DOMINI CIƆ IƆ C XXI FEBRUAR XIX

Sacred to his memory. I was Sir Henry Savile,
Warden of Merton College, Provost of Eton College. It would be in vain
to seek here for the remains of his body. Eton keeps it as a most noble
deposit. This stone holds the perennial memory of the virtues and
benefactions with which he embraced both colleges and especially the
University of Oxford and by which he has the world itself in his debt
and also the affections of his most devoted wife.
Margaret his most compliant wife placed it in honour of his deserts, she
who from a sense of duty went against his wishes in this one respect alone,
in setting up [this memorial]. He died on 19 February 1621.

Sir Henry Savile (1549–1621) was elected Fellow of Merton in 1565
and Warden in 1585. He became Provost of Eton as well in 1596. He
was a contemporary of Sir Thomas Bodley, and the founder of the
Savilian Professorships of geometry and astronomy. His monument
rivals in grandeur that of Sir Thomas Bodley, in a corresponding
position on the other side of the window.

At the end of the north transept of the ante-chapel:

COLLEGII MERTONENSIS
CUSTODI SOCIISQUE
VV. DOCTISSIMIS ET SANCTISSIMIS
A QUIBUS
CUM OXONIAM INVISERET
LIBERALI HOSPITIO RECEPTUS ERAT
HOC VAS
E LAPIDE SIBERIANO FACTUM
MEMORIS GRATIQUE ANIMI SPECIMEN
D.D.
ALEXANDER OMNIUM RUSSIARUM IMPERATOR
ANNO SACRO MDCCCXVI

Alexander, Emperor of all the Russias,
made the gift of this vase made of Siberian stone
as a token of happy memories and of gratitude
to the Warden and Fellows of Merton College,
men most learned and venerable,
by whom, when he was visiting Oxford,
he was received with generous hospitality
in 1816.

This unusual and handsome work of art has been placed in the chapel. The text in Russian appears on the other side of the plinth.

The Tsar, whose portrait hangs in the Examination Schools, came to Oxford with the King of Prussia and other grandees to receive honorary degrees from the Duke of Wellington as Chancellor at the end of the Napoleonic Wars.

The abbreviation at the beginning of the third line of the inscription is presumably to indicate *viris* (plural).

NEW COLLEGE

A small bronze plaque on the wall of the north cloister,
just before coming to one of the medieval statues
removed from the spire of St Mary's Church:

EPITAPHIUM RICHARDI DYKE HEREFORDIENSIS,
ARTIUM MAGISTRI, HUJUS COLLEGII CAPELLANI

HIC JACET IN FOSSA FOSSAE QUI NOMEN HABEBAT,
ET TUMULUM, MULTOS QUI TUMULAVIT, HABET.
OCTO SACELLANUM VIDERUNT LUSTRA RICHARDUM,
RE SENIOR SENIOR NOMINE DICTUS ERAT,
UTQUE SENEX LONGO RERUM USU, MORIBUS, ANNIS,
SIC FUIT INNOCUA SIMPLICITATE PUER.
PRISCARUM VALEAT SINCERA RELATIO RERUM,
ANNALES NOSTRAE JAM PERIERE DOMUS.
EXIIT E VITA CUM FEBRUUS EXIIT, ANNUM
SI CUPIS, ETMORBUM SCIRE DABIT **MEDICV**S
ROBERTUS LLOYD POSUIT 1604

*Funeral verses for Richard Dyke, a Herefordshire man,
Master of Arts, chaplain of this college.*

*Here lies in a ditch one who bore the name of 'ditch', and he who
buried many has his own mound. For eight times five years Richard
served the chapel. Senior in fact, he was Senior in title. And though
he was old in long experience, in character and in years, he was a
child in his innocent simplicity. Farewell, honest stories of old times;
the annals of our house have vanished now. He left life when
February ended. If you wish to know the year and illness,
his doctor will tell you.
Robert Lloyd placed this in 1604.*

The last word of the last line provides a chronogram for that year.*

---

* *Vide* p. 75 for an explanation of *lustra* and p. 76 for that of chronogram.

NUFFIELD COLLEGE

On the right of the doorway leading to
Staircase C in the upper quadrangle:

HUNC LAPIDEM POSUIT
EDWARDUS COMES DE HALIFAX
ACADEMIAE OXON. CANCELLARIUS
DIE XXI MENS. APR. A.D. MCMXLIX
ADSISTENTE WILLELMO
VICE COMITE DE NUFFIELD
AUCTORE FAUTORE CONDITORE

Edward, Earl of Halifax, Chancellor of the University of Oxford,
set this stone on the 21st day of the month of April 1949,
with William, Viscount Nuffield, the proposer,
patron and founder beside him.

William Morris (1887–1963) was created Viscount Nuffield in 1938
and gave much of the vast fortune he had made in the car industry in
the city of his birth to the university. In 1937 he endowed the future
Nuffield College, which was built after the second world war on the
site of the basin of the Oxford Canal and completed in 1960. In 1963
it became a full college of the university devoted to advanced study
and research in the social sciences.

He had endowed several chairs in the university and his generosity
extended to other colleges which then needed support. In 1943 the
Nuffield Foundation for medical, scientific and social research was
established, and in 1950 the former Wingfield Convalescent Home was
transformed into the nationally famous Nuffield Orthopaedic Centre.

The title, which is now extinct, was taken from the village of
Nuffield in the Chiltern hills on the Oxford road, some five miles
north-west of Henley-on-Thames. Nuffield Place, his home for many
years, was given to Nuffield College. The house and grounds have
now been opened to the public by the National Trust, preserved in
the manner in which they were kept in Viscount Nuffield's lifetime.

ORIEL COLLEGE

On the east wall of the Robinson building
in the middle quadrangle:

AD DEI GLORIAM ET BONARUM LITERARUM PROFECTUM
JOHANNES ROBINSON S.T.P. EPISC LOND. HORTANTE
MARIA NUPER CONJUGE EJUS AMANTISSIMA ET PROPRIO
ERGA ORIELENSES AFFECTU MOTUS HOC AEDIFICIUM F.F.
ET TRES EXHIBITIONES FUNDAVIT A.D. MDCCXIX

To the glory of God and the advancement of learning John Robinson,
Doctor of Divinity, Bishop of London, erected this building and founded
three Exhibitions. He was moved to do so through the persuasion of Mary,
his late and most loving wife, and by his own goodwill towards Oriel 1719.

One of the meanings of 'Exhibition' is that of pecuniary assistance
given to a student. It was used in this sense at Oriel, which remained
until 1838 the only example of a college in Oxford where there were
no Scholars on the foundation. The majority *in statu pupillari* were
communarii—'commoners' who received 'commons' of food on a
regular basis. Some of these gave part-time service as 'servitors', and
the corresponding role of the Bible Clerk is still to be found today
in Oxford. An undergraduate who receives an award from a college
today has the status of Exhibitioner below that of Scholar. Awards
are now usually made at the beginning of the second year based on
results in the first Public Examination.

There is a Runic line beneath the plaque, of which the meaning
is said to be 'Man is but dust.'

From the porch of St Mary's can be read:

E **LARGA MVNIFICENTIA CAECILII** RHODES

A chronogram (1911)* on the High Street frontage of Oriel records
that this building was the outcome of the great generosity of Cecil
Rhodes (1853–1902) who entered the college in 1874 and was given
an honorary degree by the university in 1899.

---

* For an explanation of the chronogram *vide* p. 76.

THE QUEEN'S COLLEGE

On the globe of the brass lectern in the chapel:

AQUILA REGINA AVIUM ET AVIS REGINENSIUM.
JOHAN. PETTIE SOCIUS COLL. MORIENS LEGAVIT AD 1653

The eagle is the queen of birds and the bird of the men of Queen's.
John Petty, Fellow of the college, made this bequest
at his death in 1653.

And on the moulded stem at the foot of the lectern:

GULIELMUS BORROGES LONDINI ME FECIT AD 1662

William Burroughes of London made me in 1662.

This splendid specimen of a seventeenth-century eagle-type lectern is one of several in the colleges. The inscription is especially appropriate for a college which bears the arms of its founder in 1341, Robert Eglesfield, with three eagles on the shield. They had originally been granted as an allusion to his family name.

The founder of *Aula Reginae de Oxonia* (the Hall of the Queen in Oxford) was chaplain to Queen Philippa, wife of King Edward III who became its patroness. The reigning Queens Consort of England have continued the patronage.

The college was wholly rebuilt at the beginning of the eighteenth century, and when the chapel was consecrated in 1719 the lectern was transferred. A statue of Queen Caroline, wife of George II, as the contemporary patroness, was set in the cupola above the new frontage in 1734.

Unlike Queens' College at Cambridge, which had two royal founders, this is known as The Queen's College.

ST EDMUND HALL

Above the entrance to the chapel on the east side of the quadrangle:

**DEO OPT. MAX.
CAPELLAM HANC SUMTU
SUO ET AMICORUM POSUIT
STEPHANUS PENTON S.T.B.
ISTIUS AULAE PRINCIPALIS
A.D. MDCLXXXII**

*To God, the Best and Greatest, Stephen Penton,
Bachelor of Theology, Principal of this Hall, built this chapel
at his own expense and that of his friends 1682.*

On the south side of the quadrangle:

**HOC EXTRUCTUM EST AEDIFICIUM
ANNIS POST SEPTINGENTIS
QUAM SANCTUS EDMUNDUS IN ABINGDONIA
PRIMUS IPSE OXONIENSIUM
ARCHIEPISCOPUS CANTUARIENSIS
EST CONSECRATUS MCCXXXIV–MCMXXXIV**

*This building was erected seven hundred years after
St Edmund of Abingdon was consecrated Archbishop of
Canterbury, the first from Oxford. 1234–1934.*

'The Hall' takes its name from St Edmund of Abingdon who, it is said, taught pupils on this site at the end of the twelfth century. He was canonised in 1246, and this has been remembered in a chronogram* (1246) over the entrance from Queen's Lane in which he is described as its luminary.

SANCTVS EDMVNDVS HVIVS AVLAE LVX

Saint Edmund, the Light of this Hall.

---

* For an explanation of the chronogram *vide* p. 76.

ST HUGH'S COLLEGE

On a sundial in the garden:

ANNIE MARY ANNE HENLEY ROGERS
CUSTOS HORTULORUM MCMXXVII–MCMXXXVII

FLORIBUS ANNA TUIS FAVEAT SOL LUCE PERENNI

Annie Mary Anne Henley Rogers
Keeper of the Gardens 1927–1937

Anna, may the sun favour thy flowers with perpetual light.

Annie Rogers (1856–1937) devoted her life to the cause of the improvement of the position of women in the University. She was for 27 years the untiring and successful secretary of the AEW—the Association for the Education of Women, who were allowed to proceed to degrees for the first time in 1920. Until then their studies had been unrecognised and unrewarded. She was a graduate of the Oxford Home Students—*Societas mulierum Oxoniae privatim studentium*—the title formally adopted in 1898, which became in 1942 St Anne's Society, and by incorporation in 1952 St Anne's College. Annie Rogers, who taught classics there until 1926, remained as Secretary to its Delegates until 1934. Her association with St Hugh's had been equally continuous as a member of its Council until 1927, when her interest in its gardens was rewarded with the appointment commemorated on the sundial.

Custos hortulorum has since remained the official designation of the Fellow responsible for the garden and grounds. The inscription was composed by Dr J.N.L. Myres. See also page 70.

ST JOHN'S COLLEGE

A brass plate in memory of Archbishop William Laud in the college chapel on the south wall behind the sedilia in the sanctuary;

IN HAC CISTULA CONDUNTUR EXUVIAE GULIELMI LAUD
ARCHIEPISCOPI CANTUARIENSIS, QUI SECURI PERCUSSUS
IMMORTALITATEM ADIIT DIE DECIMO JANUARII ANNO
DOMINI 1645⁴ AETATIS AUTEM SUAE 72 ARCHIEPISCOP. II

QUI FUI IN EXTREMIS FORTUNAM EXPERTUS UTRAMQUE
NEMO MAGIS FOELIX ET MAGE NEMO MISER.
JAM PORTUM INVENI, FLUITANTIA SECLA VALETE.
LUDITE NUNC ALIOS. PAX ERIT ALTA MIHI.

MEMORIAE DOMINI SUI IN AETERNUM HONORANDI
POSUTT GUIL. DELL SERVUS MOESTISSIMUS

In this coffin are preserved the remains of William Laud
Archbishop of Canterbury, who was beheaded and entered immortality
on the tenth day of January in the year of our Lord 1645
in his seventy-second year, the eleventh of his archiepiscopate.

One who in extremes has tasted fortune good and bad
No man more happy, none more wretched,
Now a haven I have found. Unstable time farewell.
Make ye now sport of others. Profound will be my peace.

To the memory of his master forever to be honoured
William Dell, a most grieving servant, placed [this].

The first passage is a copy of the words on the plate of Laud's leaden coffin in the crypt of All Hallows Berkyngechirche near the Tower after his execution on 10 January 1645. At the foot of the memorial William Dell, who may have composed the elegaiac couplets above, describes himself as Laud's servant. It seems likely that he entered Laud's service in St John's College as secretary to the President and remained such until the death of the Archbishop. There is no record of the provision of the brass, which is placed near the vault under the altar, in which Laud's remains were reinterred on 24 July 1663.

On a painted board on the wall of the first flight of
the buttery staircase overlooking St Giles:

SCIANT PRAESENTES ET FUTURI QUOD IN HIS CAMERIS
ALMI COLLEGII D. JO. BAPT. PER SEX FERME ANNOS
BARBARAE TRIBULATIONIS MCMXL—MCMXLV MULTI TAM
VIRI QUAM FEMINAE PROVISIONI ET DISTRIBUTIONI
CIBORUM AD SUSTENTATIONEM POPULI GRATO ANIMO
VIRES INTENDEBANT

FECERUNT BONA IN MALO TEMPORE
ET SPERAVERUNT IN PERICULOSO

Let present and future generations know that in these rooms of this
bountiful college of St John the Baptist through nearly six years of
barbarian tribulation between 1940 and 1945 men and women alike
applied their efforts with goodwill to the provision and distribution
of foods for the welfare of the nation.

They did good things in evil times
and kept up hope in time of peril.

This inscription was composed by Dr J.N.L. Myres CBE (1902–1989),
a Student of Christ Church from 1928 and Bodley's Librarian from
1948 to 1965. He served in the wartime Ministry of Food and for its
last three years of occupation of St John's College as the head of its
Fruit and Vegetable Products division. His ready Latin style is evident
in other modern inscriptions in Oxford (*vide* p. 76).

Although at its foundation in the reign of Queen Mary the
title of the college was *Sancti Johannis Baptistae*, the first word was
subsequently and unusually changed to *Divi.* (divine).

The last sentence of the inscription echoes words in English commemorating the building of Staunton Harold church in Leicestershire
recording that 'when all things sacred were throughout the nation
either demolished or profaned Sir Robert Shirley, Baronet founded
this church', which was built in 1653.

In the west cloister of the Canterbury Quadrangle,
on either side of the entrance:

E COLL. DI. JO. BAPT. OXON.
HAE TABULAE COMMEMORANT SOCIOS ALUMNOS
FAMULOS HUJUSCE COLLEGII QUI SPE AETATE INGENIO
FLORENTES NON SIBI SED PATRIAE SESE GENITOS
ARBITRATI MILITIAE ANIMOS REDDIDERUNT
A.D. MCMXIV—MCMXVIII

*These tablets commemorate the Fellows, the undergraduates and the
servants of the College of St John the Baptist in Oxford who at the peak of
their promise, youth and ability gave up their lives on military service,
considering themselves to be born not for self but for country 1914–1918.*

In the east cloister, on either side of the gate into the garden:

GRATI RECORDAMINI HUJUS COLLEGII SCHOLARES
COMMENSALES FAMULUM QUI DOMI FORISQUE
MARI TERRA AERE PATRIAE SALUTEM OMNIUM
LIBERTATEM DEFENDENTES VITAM REDDIDERUNT
ANNO DOMINI MCMXXXIX—MCMXLV

*Remember with gratitude the scholars, other undergraduates and a
member of staff of this college who at home and abroad, at sea on land and
in the air, gave up their lives defending the safety of their fatherland and
the freedom of all 1939–1945.*

In the west cloister, at its northern end:

MEMORIAE SACRUM
GULIELMI CONRAD COSTIN
SOCII TUTORIS PRAESIDIS OPTIME DE COLLEGIO MERITI
MDCCCXCIII   MCMLXX

*Sacred to the memory of William Conrad Costin, who as Fellow, Tutor
and President deserved of the college exceeding well 1893–1970.*

In the Groves above a gate leading to the President's garden:

**EDWARDUS SPROT HUJUS COLL. SOCIUS
HUNC MURUM SUIS IMPENSIS STRUXIT 1613**

*Edward Sprot, Fellow of this college,
built this wall at his own expense in 1613.*

The wall divides the President's existing garden from the former Fellows' garden. The benefactor had died in 1612 and the 'expense' was a legacy under his will. And on the right of the gate on a memorial:

FORTUNATUS ET ILLE DEOS QUI NOVIT AGRESTES

Happy too is the man who has discovered the gods of the countryside.
(Virgil, *Georgics* 2.493)

This memorial was erected in honour of the Revd H.J. Bidder who as a Fellow was *Custos silvarum* (Keeper of the Groves) for very many years.

In the corner of the rock garden, which was first laid out by Mr Bidder in the latter half of the nineteenth century, is an inscription over the doorway recording its reconstruction in 1986. On the other side of the door (always locked) is an inscription in Greek:

ΟΜΟΝΟΙΑΣ ΑΘΑΝΑΤΟΥ ΠΥΛΗ
The gate of undying harmony.

In order to see this inscription, leave the garden by a door behind the further end of the Rockery and follow the wall round to the left.

These words are copied from an archway in Marathon where the estate of Herodes Atticus (AD 101–177), a patron of the arts and a generous benefactor, bordered that of an heiress, Annia Regilla, who became his wife.

Inside the new lodge, giving access to the college from Parks Road:

OECONO**MI**AE R**V**RAL**I**S ATRIA
COLLEGIO **DIVI I**OHANNIS BAPTISTAE
ATTRIB**V**TA
OPEQ**V**E E**IV**S RESTR**VC**TA
HOSPES **IN**IS

Guest, you are now entering the Rural Economy Quadrangle
made over to the College of St John the Baptist
and rebuilt at its own expense.

This inscription records the latest extension in the large area fortunately owned by St John's, with a new entry to the college from Parks Road. The original frontage of the building erected in 1907 for Agricultural Science has been preserved. This was transferred in 1914 to a School of Rural Economy, which was founded to develop the work in accordance with contemporary requirements of the Professorship, founded in memory of Dr John Sibthorp in 1796 and associated with the College. With a new arrangement of departments within the faculty of Biological Sciences this part of the college's property became available for redevelopment, and opportunity has been taken to satisfy the need for more accommodation and large public rooms for meetings, lectures and other occasions.

As a reminder of the use of the site in recent years the courtyard between the new Garden Quadrangle and the surviving part of the 1907 frontage is known as the Rural Economy Quadrangle. The Latin word—*atrium*—has been retained for the nomenclature of interior spaces open to the sky.

The inscription (1993) is a chronogram.* In this case the differential lettering appears in the college colours of red and gold. As these cannot be reproduced in this book, the significant letters have been reproduced in bold type.

---

* For an explanation of the chronogram *vide* p. 76.

ST PETER'S COLLEGE

In the vestibule of the Morris Building—No IV staircase in
the northwest corner of the college—beneath a portrait bust:

VI SEP MDCCCL   VIII JAN MCMXXXIV
AD MEMORIAM MATRIS SUAE
AEMILIAE ANNAE MORRIS
ET IN USUM AULAE NOSTRAE
HOC AEDIFICIUM EXSTRUENDUM CURAVIT
WILLELMUS BARO NUFFIELD JUR. CIV. DOC.
FILIUS A MATRIS PIETATE
BENEVOLENTIAE EXEMPLUM TRAHENS
MCMXXXIV

*To the memory of his mother, Emily Anne Morris (1850–1934),
and for the use of our Hall, William Lord Nuffield DCL,
a son who derived the example of benevolence from the
good deeds of his mother, provided this building.*

This is the earliest example of the Rt. Hon. Lord Nuffield's benefactions to Oxford. As Sir William R. Morris, Baronet (1929) he had
been ennobled in 1934 and was to become Viscount in 1938. He had
received an Honorary Doctorate of Civil Law from the university in
1931 and could speak of 'our Hall' as a member of its Council. Details
of his post-war munificence can be found in the entry for Nuffield
College (*vide* p. 50).

The original premises of St Peter's Hall included the parochial
buildings of St Peter-le-Bailey and part of the old New Inn Hall.
The Morris Building was at first completely detached from the other
buildings but has now become part of an inner quadrangle.

UNIVERSITY COLLEGE

Beneath the statue of Dr John Radcliffe
in the eastern Radcliffe quadrangle:

**EN INTRA SUA MOENIA VOTIVA RADCLIVUM
QUI COLLEGIUM HOC
DIVINO INGENIO ALUMNUS OLIM ORNAVIT
BENEVOLENTIA DEIN QUOD VIXIT SUMMA FOVIT
MUNIFICENTIA PARI MORIENS AMPLIFICAVIT**

*Behold Radcliffe within the walls he promised to build—he,
who once, as a student, adorned this college with his godlike genius,
then fostered it with great kindness all his life, and finally,
with like munificence, made it greater at his death.*

Beneath the Latin inscription is an addition—'Presented by Dr
Radcliffe's Trustees 1719.' John Radcliffe (1652–1714) matriculated in
1665 and became Fellow of Lincoln in 1675, where he took a degree
in medicine. After 1684 he practised as a doctor so successfully in
London in the reigns of two Queens, Mary II and Anne (whose
statues appear on the High Street frontage) that he amassed a large
fortune which he left to the university. This was administered by
his trustees, who in accordance with his will provided in 1749 the
Camera, the Infirmary in 1758 and in 1794 the Observatory, now
incorporated in Green Templeton College, all of which bear the
name of this great benefactor. So does the John Radcliffe hospital,
as well as the new Radcliffe Observatory Quarter on the site of the
old Radcliffe Infirmary.

A plaque in the University Church of St Mary the Virgin records
that Dr John Radcliffe was buried on 3 December 1714 at the east
end of the north aisle.

WADHAM COLLEGE

A wall plaque above the entrance to the hall
beneath the statues of the joint founders of the college:

HOSPES
QUAM VIDES DOMUM MUSIS
NUNCUPATAM PONENDAM MANDABAT
NICHOLAS WADHAM SOMERSETENSIS
ARMIGER VERUM ILLE FATO PRAERUPTUS
DOROTHEAE CONJUGI PERFICIENDAM
LEGABAT ILLA INCUNCTANTER PERFECIT
MAGNIFICEQUE SUMPTIBUS SUIS AUXIT.
TU SUMME PATER ADSIS PROPITIUS
TUOQUE MUNERI ADDAS QUAESUMUS
PERPETUITATEM

*Visitor, Nicholas Wadham, a gentleman of Somerset,
was ordering the construction of the house for the Muses
which you see, but when he was carried off prematurely by fate
entrusted it to Dorothy his wife to complete, which she did without
delay and made splendid additions at her own expense. We pray
thee, almighty Father, to look on it with favour and grant it,
in addition to thy gift, unending life.*

Nicholas Wadham died in 1609. This foundation stone was set in its
present position according to two semicircular tablets above on 20
April 1613 *sub auspiciis R. Jacobi* (under the auspices of King James).
In the meantime Dorothy Wadham had drawn up the statutes and
appointed the first Warden.

WOLFSON COLLEGE

In the garden on a stone plinth provided for the pinnacle:

TRADIDIT HUNC LAPIDEM LYCIDAE MERTONIA DONUM
PLUS MANEAT SAXO ROBUR AMICITIAE

Merton passed on this gift to Lycidas.
May the strength of friendship last longer than stone.

The four intermediate stone pinnacles on the fifteenth-century tower of the chapel of Merton were for reasons of safely replaced about 1930. One was acquired by the University of Virginia and the remains of another stand at the eastern end of the terrace walk in Merton College garden. A third came to Wolfson about the time of its re-establishment in 1978 on the banks of the Cherwell, where it is now a feature of the attractive gardens on the south side of the new buildings.

This distich records the pleasant association established between the 'House of Scholars of Merton' founded in 1264, and settled in Oxford by 1274, and a new college of the university which seven centuries later was then its most recently created Society.

Lycidas is a Greek name, literally meaning 'Son of Wolf', used in classical contexts by Wolfson College. It is also the name of the college magazine.

A sundial in the Chinese Garden, which was presented by Sir Henry Fisher, Warden from 1975 to 1985, bears the inscription on an engraved octagonal plate—*Inter silvas Academi quaerere verum*—'to hunt for truth in the groves of Academe' (Horace, *Epistles* 2.2.45).

THE CHURCH OF
ST ALDATE

On a brass plate with the kneeling figure of a young man in a gown at a prayer desk on a pillar on the west wall in the north aisle:

IN OBITUM OPTIMAE SPEI JUVENIS ARTHURI STRODE
DEVONIENSIS NUPERRIME IN MEDIO TEMPLO LONDINIENS.
LEGUM STUDIOSI IN AULA LATE-PORTENS.
VITAM CONSUMMANTIS 23 AUGUSTI ANNO
SALUTIS 1612 AETATIS SUAE 23

EPITAPHIUM
NON JACET UT RELIQUI ARTHURUS PRAE MARMORE
CLARUS,
QUANQUAM PRAE RELIQUIS HUNC MERUISSE CANAM.
ILLOS DEFUNCTOS SUA NOBILITARE SEPULCHRA,
ATTAMEN ILLE SUUM NOBILITAT TUMULUM.

*For the death of a young Devonian of the greatest promise,
Arthur Strode, lately of London and the Middle Temple and a
student of law in Broadgates Hall, who reached the goal of life
at the age of 23 on 23 August 1612.*

An epitaph

*Arthur lies not like the rest made famous by marble, although I
celebrate him for deserts above those of the rest. Their tombs have
ennobled them in their death, yet he ennobles his own monument.*

Broadgates Hall (*Aula Late-portensis*), one of eight academic halls surviving at the end of the sixteenth century, was replaced in 1624 by the foundation of Pembroke College. Its present Senior Common Room at the north west corner of the Old Quadrangle was part of the previous building.

Until its new quadrangle was built in 1728–1732, St Aldate's Church served as a chapel for the former hall and present college.

The unusual dedication of this church has been thought to be a corruption of 'old gate' because it was near the former south entrance to the city.

THE CHURCH OF
ST GILES

On the north wall of the chancel beyond the altar rails:

HIC DORMIT CERTAM EXPECTANS RESUSCITATIONEM
ADOLESCENS MORIBUS AC VIRTUTIBUS AMABILIS
SAMUEL BUSH COLL. S. JOHN. BAPT. SOC. PROBAT. QUI
POSTQUAM IN JOHANNENSIUM SOCIETATEM CIVIUM
BRISTOLENSIUM SUFFRAGIO NUPERRIME COOPTATUS
ESSET VARIOLARUM CONFLUENTIUM FURORI SUCCUBUIT
NOV. XVII MDCCXXXI ANNO PROBATIONIS ACADEMIAE
PRIMO HUMANAE DECIMO OCTAVO

*Here sleeps Samuel Bush, a young man beloved for his manners
and worth, in the sure expectation of rising again. As a
probationary Fellow of St John Baptist College, to which he had
lately been elected by the citizens of Bristol, he would have been
brought into its Fellowship had he not fallen victim to the fury of
confluent smallpox on 17 November 1731 in his eighteenth year and
the first of his life at the university.*

Samuel Bush came up to Oxford in the Trinity Term 1731 and
was dead within six months from a fatal disease. His father being
an apothecary would have known that the mortality rate for the
'confluent' variety of *variola* (smallpox) was exceptionally high.

The third word of the inscription will be seen to *beacetam*. There has
been some error by the *lapicida* (stonecutter). A word of similar length
and appearance but more relevance has been substituted, cf. the phrase
'a sure and certain hope of the Resurrection' in the prayer of committal
in the Order for the Burial of the Dead in the *Book of Common Prayer*.

Sir Thomas White, the founder of St John's College, had been
Lord Mayor of London and was associated with several other places
in England. For that reason there were closed scholarships which
could lead to life fellowships from the Merchant Taylors' School in
London and from the historic grammar schools at Bristol, Coventry,
Reading and Tonbridge.

ST MARY MAGDALEN

A marble tablet on the west wall of the south chapel:

JUXTA SITUS EST
COMPTONUS VERNEY COLL. BALL.
COMMENSALIS, RICHARDI VERNEY
DE KINGSTON ARMIGERI IN
COMITATU WARWICENSI
FILIUS ET HAERES.
MAJORUM GENERE ILLUSTRIS,
MORUM SUAVITATE INSIGNIS,
PULCHER INGENIO, FACILIS ELOQUIO,
AD MAGNA NATUS
A DIVO AD MELIORA RAPTUS
ANNO { AETATIS SUAE 19
{ SALUTIS 1689
DIE 12 SEPTEMBRIS

*Near here lies Compton Verney, gentleman commoner of
Balliol College, son and heir of Richard Verney, Gentleman,
of Kingston in the county of Warwickshire. Distinguished in the
line of his ancestors, renowned for his agreeable manners, of fine
intellect, ready speech, born to great things but snatched away
by God to a better life at the age of 19 on 12 September 1689.*

Commensales, gentlemen or fellow commoners, were admitted to
colleges in the seventeenth and eighteenth centuries on payment
of high fees. For this as paying guests they received some of the
amenities provided for Fellows, with whom they could dine at High
Table. Those who were sons of noblemen wore gold tassels on their
square black caps.

The family home may have been near the King Stone, a monolith
connected with the adjoining circle of the Rollright Stones just across
the border in Warwickshire.

THE CITY CHURCH OF
ST MICHAEL AT THE NORTH GATE

In the centre of the south wall of the church:

H.S.E.
JOHANNES HARRIS CIVITATIS HUJUS
ALDERMANUS ET EXPRAETOR DIGNISSIMUS
RELIGIONI REGI AC PATRIAE
PESSIMIS ETIAM TEMPORIBUS FIDUS.
NATUS BURFORDIAE ANNO 1594
DENATUS OXONIAE 1674 AETATIS 80
UTRIUSQUE LOCI PAUPERIBUS AD
OCTINGENTAS LIBRAS LIBERALIS
QUA MUNIFICENTIA TANTA
MONUMENTUM SIBI POSUIT MARMORE OMNI PERENNIUS
LEGE, BONE CIVIS ET IMITARI AUDE

Here is buried John Harris, a most worthy alderman and former mayor
[1663–64] of this city, faithful to his church, king and country even in the
most adverse times. Born at Burford 1594, died at Oxford 1674
in the eightieth year of his life. He was generous to the poor of both places,
giving eight hundred pounds, by which great munificence he built
a monument to himself more lasting than any marble.
Read, good citizen and resolve to copy him.

There follow details of his two wives, by the first of whom he had six daughters and three sons, the last surviving of whom erected this monument in 1675.

Exegi monumentum aere perennius—'more durable than bronze my memorial shall be'. The opening line of Horace, *Odes* III.30 was often quoted in epitaphs, *marmore* (marble) being substituted here for *aere* (bronze). There is a half-length figure monument of John Harris in the St Thomas of Canterbury chapel of Burford parish church.

The numerous monuments in the Church of St Michael at the North Gate have been made the easier to study by the provision of transcriptions of the texts and translation in calligraphic script in adjacent frames.

THE UNIVERSITY CHURCH OF
ST MARY THE VIRGIN

On the north side of a restored altar tomb in the north chapel:

HIC JACET DOMINUS ADAM DE BROME — QUONDAM
CLERICUS CANCELLARIAE DOMINI REGIS EDWARDI
SECUNDI — CANCELLARIUS DUNELMENSIS —
ARCHIDIACONUS DE STOW IN ECCLESIA LINCOLNENSI —
RECTOR HUJUS ECCLESIAE. — PRIMUS PRAEPOSITUS
DOMUS SCHOLARIUM BEATAE MARIAE OXONIAE
COMMUNITER COLLEGII ORIELENSIS NUNCUPATAE —
QUAM DOMUM AB EODEM ADAM INCOHATAM REX
EDWARDUS SECUNDUS MOX DENUO FUNDA VIT ET AUXIT
— QUIQUIDEM ADAM OBIIT XVI DIE MENSIS JUNII ANNO
DOMINI MCCCXXXII CUJUS ANIMAE PROPITIETUR DEUS
AMEN

And at the west end of the tomb:

HOC BENEFACTORIS SUI MONUMENTUM VICISSITUDINE
TEMPORUM QUODAMMODO DILAPSUM REPARANDUM
ET ADORNANDUM CURAVIT COLLEGIUM ORIELENSE
ANNO MCMXL

*Here lies Master Adam de Brome, sometime clerk of the Chancellery of
the Lord King Edward II, Chancellor of Durham, Archdeacon of Stow in
the Diocese of Lincoln, Rector of this Church. He was the first Provost of
the house of scholars of the Blessed Mary in Oxford commonly known as
Oriel College. Later King Edward II refounded and extended the house
begun by this same Adam, who died on 16 June 1332.
May the Lord have mercy on his soul. Amen.*

*In 1940 Oriel College undertook the repair, restoration and embellishment
of this tomb of its benefactor somewhat damaged by accidents in the past.*

With this background the college uses as its corporate designation 'The
Provost and Scholars of the House of the Blessed Mary the Virgin
in Oxford, commonly called Oriel College, of the Foundation of
Edward the Second, of famous memory, sometime King of England'.

At the east end of the north aisle of the church:

JOHANNES DUNS SCOTUS O.F.M.
QUI IN LECTURIS OXONIENSIBUS
REPRAESENTAVIT DAVIDICUM ILLUD
DOMINUS ILLUMINATIO MEA
HOC LAPIDE A FRATRIBUS SUIS
POSITO POST ANNOS SEPTINCENTOS
COMMEMORATUR   A.D. MCMLXVI

John Duns Scotus, Order of the Friars Minor, who in his
Oxford lectures displayed in reality the words of David,
the psalmist —The Lord is my Light'. This is commemorated
by this stone placed by his brethren 700 years later in 1966.

John Duns Scotus (1266–1308) is famous for his commentaries on
the Bible and was known by his contemporaries as *Doctor Subtilis* for
his criticism of the teaching of the Dominican Thomas Aquinas. He
taught also in Paris and at Cologne, where he is buried.

The Friars Minor, or Lesser Brothers, were founded by St Francis
of Assisi in 1210. Their nickname of 'Scotists' was acquired from
the area of the birth of this scholastic philosopher, and the word
'dunce' may be derived from the small town of Duns, in the county
of Berwickshire.

This memorial is placed appropriately near to the historic centre
of the university, with which the Franciscans had close links from the
thirteenth century and this is recalled by the inclusion of the motto
of the university in the inscription.

A record elsewhere in Oxford of the activity of another scholar
of the Order will be found on page 71.

On a curved stone bench in the churchyard:

UT FLOREAT MEMORIA
ANNIE MARIAE ANNAE HENLEY ROGERS A.M.
LITTERARUM ANTIQUARUM PRAECEPTRICIS
MULIERUM IURIS IN UNIVERSITATE VINDICIS
FLORUM HORTORUMQUE CULTRICIS
QUAE IN HAC AEDE DEUM FREQUENTER ADORABAT
HOC SEDILE EXSTRUXERUNT HORTULOS CIRCUM
FLORIBUS REPLEVERUNT COLENDOS IN FUTURUM
CURAVERUNT COLLEGAE ALUMNAE AMICI
MCMXXXVIII

So that a remembrance may flourish for
Annie Maria Anna Henley Rogers, M.A.,
a teacher of ancient literature, champion of the right of women
in the University, a cultivator of flowers and gardens, who
frequently used to worship God in this church, the students of her
college put out this seat and filled the little gardens around with
flowers, and took care that they would be tended in the future.
1938.

Annie Rogers was a staunch advocate of women's rights within the university (see p. 54). The university commemorated her work in 1939 with the restoration of a garden on the north side of the church of St Mary, in which she had regularly worshipped. The inscription above, carved onto a curved stone bench at the west end, pays tribute to the role she had played in the interests of women. Another inscription on the steps leading from the garden into Radcliffe Square reads:

DOMINUS CUSTODIAT INTROITUM TUUM
ET EXITIUM TUUM

May the Lord preserve thy coming in and thy going out.
(Psalm 121.8)

IN THE PARISH OF
ST EBBE

A tablet with English translation beneath,
located on a wall above a lawn at the end of
Turn Again Lane leading to Old Greyfriars Street:

ROGERUS BACON
PHILOSOPHUS INSIGNIS DOCTOR MIRABILIS
QUI METHODO EXPERIMENTALI
SCIENTIAE FINES MIRIFICE PROTULIT
POST VITAM LONGAM STRENUAM INDEFESSAM
PROPE HUNC LOCUM INTER FRANCISCANOS SUOS
IN CHRISTO OBDORMIVIT
A.S. MCCXCII

The great philosopher, Roger Bacon, known as the Wonderful Doctor,
who by the experimental method extended marvellously the realm
of knowledge and after a long life of untiring activity fell asleep
in Christ near this place among his fellow Franciscans
in 1292.

Oxford City Council provided this well-designed memorial tablet in
1917 to record the site of the convent of the Franciscan Friars who had
settled in Oxford by 1224. Roger Bacon (born *c.* 1214), who joined
them twenty years later, became Oxford's best known early scientist.
Traditionally he had a study and a laboratory over a gateway on
Grandpont (later called Folly Bridge). His *Opus Majus* led to a charge
of heresy, for which he suffered imprisonment.

Excavations in St Ebbe's between 1967 and 1976 provided evidence
about the site of the Friary of the Grey Friars, so named after the
colour of their habits, on either side of the city wall.

The Franciscans returned to Oxford in 1910 to open a house of
studies. Between 1957 and 2008 it had the status of a permanent
private hall of the university in a new building in Iffley Road known
as Greyfriars.

THE PRIORY OF THE DOMINICAN ORDER OF
BLACKFRIARS

Over the entrance door of the priory beneath a statue of the Virgin Mary on the west side of St Giles opposite St John's:

HUNC CONVENTUM ALTERUM
NOVUM EADEM DIE QUA PRISCUS
FUNDATUS EST A.D. MCCXXI
FRATRES PRAEDICATORES
LONGUM POST EXILIUM REDUCES
POSUERUNT XVIII KAL. SEPT. MCMXXI

The Friars of the Order of Preachers, back after long exile, set up this second new Priory on 15 August 1921, the same day of the year as that of their original foundation in 1221.

The Dominican Friars, whose order had been founded by St Dominic only five years before, claim to have established their house in Oxford on a site near the river in 1221. The outline of their church and priory buildings has been located by archaeologists at the south end of Littlegate Street, where an original gateway still exists within the buildings of the Deaf and Hard of Hearing Centre. The modem Blackfriars Road and Preachers Lane mark the other side of the site. This first priory was suppressed in 1538.

The Dominican Order (O.P. for *Ordo Praedicatorum*—Order of Preachers) is especially devoted to preaching and study. Their popular name comes from a black mantle worn over a white habit. The *stadium* (seminary) of the English province of the Order within the priory of Blackfriars is a permanent private hall of the university under the direction of a Regent of Studies.

This inscription on the modern priory provides an example of the skill in lettering of Eric Gill (1882–1940) who did other such work in Oxford.

THE CHURCH OF ST MARGARET
IN THE PARISH OF BINSEY

On a well head in the churchyard a few
yards to the west of the church:

S. MARGARETAE FONTEM
PRECIBUS S. FRIDESWIDAE UT FERTUR CONCESSUM
INOPINATUM DIU OBRUTUMQUE
IN USUM REVOCAVIT
T.J. PROUT AED. XTI. ALUMNUS VICARIUS
A.D. MDCCCLXXIV

T.J. Prout, a member of Christ Church, vicar,
brought back into life the spring of St Margaret,
which it is said had been granted in answer to the prayers of
St Frideswide, but had long been unsuspected and overgrown.
1874.

The Revd Thomas Prout decided to restore the well when he became
incumbent of this Christ Church living in 1857. Alice, daughter of
Dean Liddell, was in the party which the Revd C.L. Dodgson (Lewis
Carroll) took upstream to see the 'treacle' well at Binsey about a
quarter of a mile from the River Isis (*Thamesis*) during the course of
its restoration. This provided him with ideas for the remarks of the
Dormouse in *Alice in Wonderland*, which was published in 1865.

The well acquired its name in the medieval sense of a healing
balm. It is said that St Frideswide, who founded the monastery which
became Christ Church, was pursued to Binsey by King Algar, who
was struck blind for his boldness in wanting to marry her. Her prayers
to St Margaret called forth a miraculous well whose waters cured her
suitor's blindness. In the St Frideswide window in the Latin Chapel
of the cathedral by Edward Burne-Jones in 1859, the sick and crippled
and a dog with a bandaged paw are shown on a pilgrimage to the
well house at Binsey seeking a cure.

Vicarius, from which the title of vicar is derived, means one who
acts as a substitute or deputy.

ST CLEMENT

THE VICTORIA FOUNTAIN

On the plinth on the Magdalen Bridge side of the fountain:

IN HONOREM VICTORIAE D.G. BRIT. REG.
A.D. MDCCCXCVII DUODECIM JAM LUSTRA* COMPLENTIS
FONTEM ISTUM CUM HOROLOGIO PARANDUM
CURAVIT CUM UXORE G. HERBERTUS MORRELL SENATOR

*In honour of Victoria by grace of God Queen of Great Britain
and now in 1897 completing the sixtieth year of her reign Alderman
G. Herbert Morrell and his wife presented this fountain and clock.*

On the smaller of the two islands in the middle of the Plain stood between 1771 and 1869 a turnpike toll-house close to the west end of the old church of St Clement. It controlled one road on each side leading to and from Oxford. The Victoria Fountain was inaugurated on this site in 1899 in the presence of H.R.H. Princess Louise, the Duchess of Argyll. The donors were members of the Oxford family of brewers.

On eight separate tablets just below the level of the clock faces:

LYMPHA CADIT
RUIT HORA
SAGAX BIBE
CARPE FUGACEM

*The water drips, the hours go by.
Be warned, drink, catch them ere they fly.*

The Latin words though separated in pairs together constitute a hexameter line.

---

* *Vide* p. 75 for an explanation of *lustra*.

ROMAN CHRONOLOGY

THE CALENDAR

I T IS exceptional to find an undated inscription. Some include as well as the *annus* (year) in question the *dies* (day) of the *mensis* (month). Three Roman festivals—*Kalendae* (the first day of the month), *Nonae* (the fifth) and *Idus* (the thirteenth) were the basis of the rather complicated structure, which can be worked out from the instances in some of the examples provided. The principle is that of 'ante-dating', e.g. A.D. VIII. KAL. JAN. (*ante diem octavum Kalendas Januarias*) using both days involved—the eighth before the first—for 25 December. But remember that 'in March, July, October, May the Ides are on the fifteenth day' and the *Nones* therefore on the seventh.

The year on a Latin inscription is nearly always displayed in Roman numerals originally abbreviated in certain cases from words—M (mille—1000); D (500—for its origin see below); C (centum—100); L (invented for 50), then X for 10 (the symbol for *decem* on a *denarius*), V (the upper half of X) for 5, with a series of units to the amount required. All other numbers are expressed by a combination of these. A method of subtraction by reversal used for IV, reducing V by I, or XIX—one short of twenty.

The choice of D to represent 500 came through corruption of another symbol, of half of CIↃ (= Mille), of ancient usage and imitated on some inscriptions e.g. in the Ashmolean Museum (p. 16) and on the Savile monument in Merton (p. 47). Ingenious copyists combined the right-hand half of this cipher, to form D.

Another way of describing duration of years is through the use of *lustrum* (plural form—*lustra*). This was a purificatory sacrifice performed after the completion of a census every *quinquennium* (five years) which could be multiplied as necessary.

From *Kalendae* is derived the English 'calendar', which in Oxford has been used since 1809 as the title of the university directory of 'Ceremonies and Remarkable Days'. The same format has been followed to provide in the calendar for each academic year the relevant dates and reference details for the university and each college with records of graduation for the previous year. The 'Remarkable Days' became a feature of the *Oxford Almanack*, which has been published annually since 1674, the invention of Dr John Fell.

THE CHRONOGRAM

A chronogram has been defined as a sentence or verse in which certain letters express a date, while the sentence itself alludes to the event to which the date belongs. This is achieved by distinguishing appropriate letters by size or colour from the rest. Such a device requires the use of I for J and V for U, as in HVIVS instead of HUJUS. The letters J and U were lacking in the original Latin alphabet. In manuscripts and in the printed word until the end of the sixteenth century there was no recognised distinction and either form was acceptable. To avoid confusion the extended alphabet has been substituted where necessary in these texts except in the case of chronograms.

Some words could be described as chronogrammatic e.g. DUM, DUX, LUX in which every letter can count as a Roman numeral. As X is otherwise not an easy letter to introduce, its value can be provided by the substitution of two V, and likewise two L make C. It is hardly possible, however, to construct sentences which contain the numerical values in their correct sequence.

Examples are to be found soon after the invention of printing and there seems to have been a revival of this conceit in Oxford as a *jeu d'esprit*. Four examples are provided in the selected texts at New College (p. 49) at Oriel (p. 51), at St Edmund Hall (p. 53), and at St John's (p. 59). Other chronograms are to be found above the entrance of Frewin Hall off New Inn Hall street, recording that C.L. Shadwell, later Provost of Oriel, lived there in 1881, and on a plaque above a basement window of the former Dyson Perrins Laboratory (now the Oxford University Centre for the Environment) designed by Paul Waterhouse in 1914 in South Parks Road. This latter is worth quotation in view of its humorous and self-depreciative content: BALLIOLENSIS FECI HYDATOECVS O SI MELIVS—'I, Waterhouse of Balliol, did this. Oh, if only it were better.' A more elaborate arrangement using two colours, red and blue, is a feature of exceptional interest at the north west end of the Upper Reading Room of the Bodleian Library to record the date of reconstruction when a new partition wall was made to form the end of the room in 1954. Dr

J.N.L. Myres, Bodley's Librarian at that time, the composer of the two elegant couplets of the inscription, 'thought that such a piece of learned nonsense would be in tune with the *Zeitgeist* of Renaissance Oxford which took great pleasure in verbal Latin conceits of this kind.'* The device was used again in the cornice of the Selden End of Duke Humfrey's library in 1967, but only admitted Readers have the opportunity to see these.

On the north side of the great gateway into the Botanic Garden are four quotations from the Old Testament in Hebrew to mark the site of the former Jewish burial ground. Some of the numeral letters are marked with arrows so as to indicate the year 1290, in which the Jews were expelled from Oxford.

---

* *Vide* D.R. Howlett, *The Bodleian Record Vol XIV.*5 (October 1993) pp. 446–8. 'Bodley Librarian's Learned Nonsense'.

SOME EPIGRAPHIC
ABBREVIATIONS

A.C.	*Anno Christ*—In the year of Christ
ACAD.	*Academia*—University
A.D.	*Anno Domini*—In the year of Our Lord
A.M.	*Artium magister*—Master of Arts, more commonly M.A.
A.M.D.G.	*Ad majorem Dei gloriam*—To the greater glory of God
ARM.	*Armiger*—Gentleman
A.S.	*Anno Sacro/Salutis*—In the holy year/year of salvation
B.M.	*Bene meritofmerenti*—Well deserved
C.V.	*Clarissimus vir*—Distinguished man
CLER.	*Clericus*—In holy orders
COLL.	*Collegium*—College
D.D.	*Donum/dono dedit/dederunt*—Gave as a gift
D.G.	*Dei gratia*—By grace of God
D.M.	*Dis manibus*—To the spirit (of the dead)
D.O.M.	*Deo optima maximo*—To God, the best and greatest
ECCL.	*Ecclesia*—Church
EPI.	*Episcopus*—Bishop
F.F.	*Fecit/fecerunt/fieri*—Had made
FAC. CUR.	*Faciendum curavit*—Caused to be built
FIL.	*Filius*—Son
H.J.	*Hic jacet*—Here lies
H.S.E.	*Hic situs est*—Here is buried
I.M.	*In memoriam*—In memory of
IMP.	*Imperator*—King/Emperor
MIL.	*Miles*—Knight
M.S.	*Sacrum memoriae*—Sacred to the memory of
OB.	*Obiit*—Died
P.C.	*Ponendum/poni curavit*—Caused to be placed
P.M.	*Piae memoriae*—To the affectionate memory of
P.P.	*Pie posuit*—Dutifully placed
PR.	*Presbyter*—Priest
R.P.	*Respublica*—The State
S.T.P.	*Sanctae Theohgiae Professor*—Doctor of Divinity (D.D.)
SOC.	*Socius/Societas*—Fellow/Fellowship
VIX.	*Vixit*—Lived

INDEX

79